GREAT BLUE

GREAT BLUE
Odyssey of a Heron

by
Marnie Reed Crowell

Threehalf Press

Originally published by TIMES BOOKS, a division of
Quadrangle/The New York Times Book Co., Inc.
Three Park Avenue, New York, N.Y. 10016

Published simultaneously in Canada by Fitzhenry &
Whiteside, Ltd., Toronto

Reissued 2011

by Threehalf Press, Sunset, ME 04683

Library of Congress Cataloging in Publication Data

Crowell, Marnie Reed. Great Blue.

I. Great blue heron. I. Title.
QL696.C52C76 598'.34 79-91666

ISBN 978-0-9802177-5-9

Manufactured in the United States of America

For Ken

THE FLIGHT

The Route of Great Blue

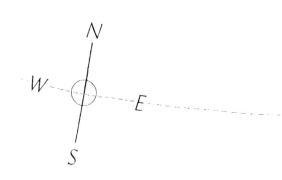

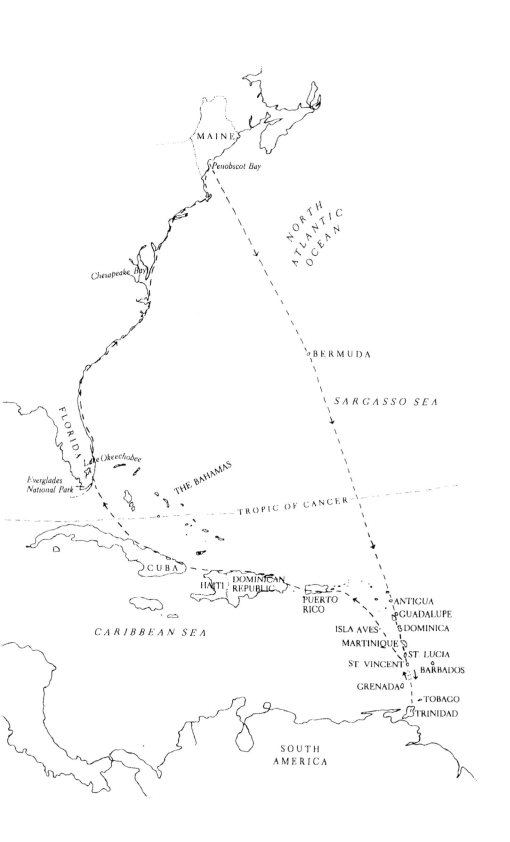

MAINE

Penobscot Bay

NORTH ATLANTIC OCEAN

Chesapeake Bay

BERMUDA

SARGASSO SEA

FLORIDA

Lake Okeechobee

Everglades National Park

THE BAHAMAS

TROPIC OF CANCER

CUBA

DOMINICAN REPUBLIC

HAITI

PUERTO RICO

CARIBBEAN SEA

ANTIGUA

GUADALUPE

ISLA AVES

DOMINICA

MARTINIQUE

ST. LUCIA

ST. VINCENT

BARBADOS

GRENADA

TOBAGO

TRINIDAD

SOUTH AMERICA

GREAT BLUE

Odyssey of a Heron

A great blue heron and its young

1
MAINE

ON A PLATFORM OF sticks high in the top of a spruce tree sat a great blue heron. She was the color of the sea at dawn. Beneath her breast lay five large eggs with shells of ancient blue-green, nearly ready to hatch. She ruffled the feathers of her huge wings and drew them closer about her. Spread, her wings spanned a full six feet. Her powerful bill could crush almost any adversary, yet she was uneasy.

Two black forms had been stealthily slipping through the darkness of the spruces, ever closer to the big shaggy nest. Although she kept her eye on the pair of ravens hopping silently from branch to branch, they did not really worry the heron. She could handle them if they came too close. What bothered her was the boat that had crossed the bay and circled her small island several times. A man had beached the boat and was working his way through the trees where the heron nests were.

She could catch an occasional glimpse of the intruder. She was familiar with the human form, but the alien silhouette of the knapsack on his back may have contributed further to the heron's unease. However, she had never had a direct interaction with man, so she was able to sit tight. She held her head high, eyes glaring alertly, head cocked tautly. The crack of dry branches on the ground told her his footsteps were coming near. Carefully she shifted her weight over the eggs. She raised the feathers of her crest, arched her neck, stretched for one more look, and then drew her head and long neck down flat against her back.

Below her the ground was carpeted with spruce needles stained white with the droppings of all the herons which came to this island in Penobscot Bay on the coast of Maine. Here the great blue herons for miles around came to roost at night and to build their nests and raise their young.

The man who was making his way in the shadows of the spruces grimaced at the strong smell of the droppings which whitewashed the rocks and trees. Then he smiled, for he could see the heron and her nest silhouetted above him. He smiled, for he came in peace.

4

The man shifted the camera he was carrying to his shoulder and began to climb the tree beside the heron's nest. He chose this nest from all the others because it stood at the outer edge of the group of nests in the heronry. He did not wish to disturb the birds.

Slowly, the man pulled himself up from branch to branch. He proceeded cautiously, because many of the branches would not bear his weight. The lower branches had died because the sunlight no longer reached them; nearer the top of the tree the limbs had been killed by heron guano. The spruce was treacherously slippery with the wetness and the growth upon it. Nearly all the branches carried old-man's-beard, a greenish-gray lichen. It hung in wisps from the damp dark limbs; rain that never fell, flourishing in the Maine fogs.

Higher and higher climbed the man, smiling all the while at the heron. He did not see the two black ravens, darker than the shadows around them. He had eyes only for the heron on her nest.

She glared at him and flattened her body over her precious eggs a bit more. Her heart pounded against the shells.

The man inched his way along the last limb that was big enough to bear him and his camera. He sighted through his camera and thought happily about the fine photographs he would have. He loved the bay and admired the great herons he had so often watched feeding in the coves. He was delighted to have discovered the island nesting place of the great blue herons.

Awkwardly he groped behind him for the light meter he carried in his knapsack. His arm brushed a dead branch, breaking it with a loud snap.

The heron could remain frozen no longer. She exploded from the nest and wheeled away into the air in alarm. As the two hungry ravens flashed up to the unprotected nest the man watched in helpless horror. Each raven gave an egg a quick blow with its powerful beak and carried away a dripping shell.

The air rang with the disconsolate-sounding cries of the heron circling above. She could not master her fear to return to her nest.

The photographer realized it was his doing that the coast would know fewer of the wonderful great blue herons this summer. He climbed down through the clawing spruce branches, made his way back to the boat on the beach, and headed out to sea with a heavy heart. The croaking cry of a raven came across the water to mock him.

The heron spread her dusky wings to brake her flight and landed her long legs onto the edge of the plundered nest. She studied the fragments of shell and the smear of albumen that was all that remained of two of her offspring. As she settled herself gently down on the remaining eggs, she heard the first faint peeps from within them. In these eggs still beat the hearts of herons to come, and perhaps she could raise three.

A few months ago, the cold winds of April had blown across the gray waters of the bay, and patches of snow still lay in the shade of the spruces when the herons had come back from the south. Sky-blue hepaticas were blooming promises of spring. Robins were back; noisy flocks of red-winged blackbirds filled bare treetops and boiled up from barren fields. Long lines of Canada geese came honking by in the night.

In the pearly light of dawn the herons had danced together on the mud flat of the cove across from the island. At least it looked like a dance. Groups of herons—loners for most of their lives—stood near one another on the icy flats. As birds approached each other they found themselves rebuffed by mildly hostile signals. A few days later male herons chose a nest site, usually an old nest which over the years may have become quite substantial. Some, chiefly younger birds, had to accept less desirable locations in the treetops on the edge of the circle to build their rickety platforms.

Each male defended his nest vigorously against all comers, even the females. Eventually these bachelors accepted a female, but at the first, theirs was a very tense relationship. Again and again the male would stab at the face of the female, who would draw back her head just far enough to avoid his stab. If she could, the female would grab the male's bill with her own and hold it for a few seconds.

Soon these ritualized rapier duels gave way to the ceremony of bill clappering. Making a rapid clicking noise, the herons nibbled each other's backs. The female kept her eyes averted, her head low, her crest sleeked, while poking at sticks in the nest. The male's aggressiveness declined. They had become a pair.

In the early mornings and evenings of the next few days, when the female was not off foraging, the herons copulated. He walked slowly around the female, then stepped gently onto her crouching back. A bit of tail wagging, and off he flew.

Nests were improved, the male stealing sticks from his neighbors' nests and bringing them back to his female to poke into their own. Eggs were laid and incubated. The early spring flowers came and went. New leaves unfolded on the birches of the islands. Swarms of tiny insects appeared, eating the sweet nectar and pollen of the trees' flowers. Wave after wave of migrant warblers dined on the bountiful supply of insects. A few—the black-throated green, and the yellow-rumped warbler among them—stayed to raise their families in the spruces. Tiny silver-blue parula warblers began to build their nests by weaving together the strands of the old-man's-beard lichen.

On the bald, treeless island just out to sea from the herons' island, baby eider ducks were beginning to hatch. Great black-backed gulls constantly lurked around the islands in hopes of nabbing a tender duckling.

High atop the spruces the three eggs of the heron were hatching. A star-shaped hole appeared on first one egg and then another. The herons pipped their shells with a special temporary bony knob on the end of their bills.

Throughout the colony, gawky heron babies struggled one after another out of their shells and into the light of day. As they rested and dried off, the dark blood vessels throbbed under the pink and wrinkled skin of these small packages of life.

For three weeks and more the parents brooded their offspring.

When cold rains lashed the treetops and fierce winds whipped crashing waves all about the island, the parent herons sheltered the young with their own warm bodies. The young birds were more susceptible to soaking, and their little bodies were not yet able to adjust their temperature.

The summer sun rose ever higher in the sky, creating mirages in the glaring cloudless noons; the burning heat threatened to scorch the panting heron babies. One parent stood for patient hours holding out a wing to shade the young until the other came to stand a turn.

At times the nest on the edge of the heronry was silent as the downy babies slept. A few bees visited the rugosa roses that bloomed by the beach. Gentle waves lapped the shore. But more often the island was alive with the comings and goings of parent birds bringing food to their nestlings. The young would scramble, pecking and clacking their bills at each other, lunging at the huge adult standing a moment at the edge of the ring of sticks. The parent would gulp, bring up a mouthful, and regurgitate partly digested fish onto the floor of the nest. With no ceremony and no consideration for each other, the siblings would grab the pieces as fast as they could. From the time they were ten days old, competition among the siblings had reached such a pitch that the oldest, most aggressive, would seize the parent's bill crosswise in its own. Scissoring the parent's bill, the youngster would maintain that grip most vigorously against the challenges of its nest mates. It often happened that the youngest chick starved to death by the fourth week.

The young herons spent hours practicing striking at things in their nest: sticks, leaves, or the many houseflies attracted to the guano and decaying fish in the nest. They soon attained sufficient coordination between the tip of their bill and their binocular vision to become quite proficient in nabbing these moving targets.

When a youngster from a neighboring nest appeared one day, the occupants raised their little crown feathers and drove the intruder off. Soon they too began to explore the treetop world, crawling around and around their stick saucer in the sky, helping themselves along with their scrawny wings.

By hooking their oversized bills onto branches, the three herons of the outermost nest managed to pull themselves limb by limb several trees away from their own. The mummified corpse of a heron chick which had gotten caught in the dense twigs hung in the spruce shadows. The corners of the bird's outsized head had held it fast in the tangle; its legs had dangled helplessly in the air, and it had perished. The three young herons scrambled by.

From their new vantage the young herons could see the waters of the bay around them. Bright colored lobster-pot buoys were bobbing everywhere. Long ropes disappearing into the depths of the sea marked the slatted traps that waited to catch the lobsters that walked the bottom of the bay. The herons watched the sails of a few pleasure boats on the distant horizon. Across the water they could see a small fishing village where every house looked out to sea. Their world had become larger.

As the afternoon shadows lengthened, the three headed back to their nest. Tree traveling seemed to require greater effort in the fast cooling air. They heaved and pushed and pulled their way back through branches that seemed to ensnare them. The smallest, the runt who was never the first to be fed, pulled itself along as best it could while the biggest heronlet impatiently brought up the rear.

One bird scrambled onto the nest. The runt tried to pull itself to the stick platform. It reached out its head, pulled and strained, but could not quite pull across the gap. As it stretched again and struggled onto the next branch, the remaining heron swung over to another branch to go around the little bird. Hurrying onto the half-dead limb, the sturdy youngster lost its footing. Down it tumbled, down through the dark branches, down past dead and bare twigs, down to the shadowy grass below.

Two streaky-breasted young herons peered goggle-eyed over the edge of the nest.

Over on the wharf in the little fishing village two boys were passing camping gear down to their father in the waiting boat, a small outboard. The tide was low, so each box and bag had to be carried down the steep gangway that joined the floating lobster car with the stationary granite shore. What looked like decking was in fact the top of the huge floating pound that held the lobsters the fishermen brought in. A boat had tied up at the pound. Its green, claw-waving catch had been weighed in wire baskets and poured into the watery, dark storage pen beneath the boards where the boys walked. A lobsterman, in yellow oilskin apron and flapping rubber boots with the tops turned down, was loading tubs of smelly fish heads. These he would stuff into small bait bags to be threaded into his lobster traps later.

The boys and their father exchanged greetings with the lobsterman, stowed their gear, and pushed off from the dock. They headed their little boat out to sea, crossed the busy thoroughfare buzzing with lobster boats, outboards, and yachts, and skirted the granite shores of the islets dotting the harbor. Behind them the houses, most with the high-peaked roofs of Greek Revival style popular a century ago, shrank in the distance to a quaint needlepoint panorama. Sleek white lobster boats bobbed at their moorings in front of weathered fish shacks hung with bright lobster-pot buoys. The rambling sardine-canning factory sprawled out over the water on pilings. Seagulls perched on brick chimneys, wheeled screaming over the harbor, and decorated the roof of the sardine factory. Much of what an outsider took for quaintness was the raw, bare-boned simplicity of a hard way to make a living.

As the small motorboat passed a cove on one of the off islands, an osprey folded its black-and-white wings, plunging into the water with a splash. Seconds later it beat its way up into the air with a shining fish in its talons. Another osprey rose from its nest hidden in the spruces as the boat approached its island destination.

"Kree, kree, kree" the anxious birds called hovering high above, as the bow of the boat bumped the kelp-draped rocks of shore, and the boys leaped onto land.

In short order the boat was moored and the two boys followed their father up the path to the lighthouse that crowned the height of the island. A neat square white tower held aloft the gleaming prisms and handsome black ironwork of the light, but of lighthouse keeper's quarters there was none. Fire had claimed that years ago. Now only the Coast Guard periodically visited the automatic light, and visited the rhubarb patch that was all that remained of the lightkeeper's garden.

Only the Coast Guard came—and the biologist and his family who were given permission to use the island as a base for their studies of the heron rookery on the island just across the way. The island heronry, where the great birds gathered to nest, was one of only fifteen or twenty along the entire coast of Maine. The days when herons might be shot and salted for fish bait were long gone, and most people nowadays seemed to appreciate the wonderful creatures. However, being conspicuous, colonial, and shy meant great blue herons might be expected to have some difficulty adjusting to expanding human populations. Because the birds feed over a wide area and at the top of the food chain, their numbers might reflect any disturbance in the complex web of marine organisms, an indication of the health of the whole bay. So biologists wanted to know more about them.

The biologist's family had just finished unloading their supplies when a commotion from the adjacent island caught their attention. It was the heron rookery, and something was wrong. Adult birds wheeled and complained in the air above the treetops. The biologist and his boys ran down to the boat. The motor sputtered back into action. As their boat drew near, the boys could see in the nests the knobby heads of young herons waving spike bills and wailing.

They beached their boat and quickly made their way toward the nest sites. A brief reconnoiter failed to explain the birds' distress.

11

Puzzled, the man and his sons returned to the boat and began to unload it. The biologist took out a metal tool chest; the boys carried burlap bags and a coil of rope up the steep granite shoulder of the island. The tool chest, clanking at every step the biologist took, was filled with metal bird bands. As part of his study, the biologist banded young herons each spring. He had done no more than circle the island at a distance, counting the number of active nests while the herons were young and vulnerable. The birds would soon be fledged, so he had come today to get bands on the young before they left the nest.

The trio shouldered their gear and plunged into the spruces. Crouching under branches here, shouldering through there, they made their way through the thicket. The strong smell, guano spattered ground, an eggshell or two, and a moldy green bird skull told them when they stood directly beneath the heronry.

"Okay, which boy wants to climb the trees?"

Both and neither. The elder was handed a rope, canvas, sacks, a pair of goggles, and was dispatched aloft. As he climbed he thought about the scar his father had above his left eyebrow. Herons strike preferentially at eyelike patterns, an efficient adaptation for coping with would-be predators. At any rate, years ago a heron had split the neophyte investigator's brow like a ripe peach and come within a fraction of an inch of taking out his eye.

Going up the rough tree trunk was unpleasant; finding a convenient and comfortable perch near the spindly treetop was tricky. The young herons above the boy could hear him climbing and feel their tree shake. He had to be careful lest he alarm the birds so much that they scrambled out of the nest and broke their necks.

Crouching out of sight in twigs below the nest to let the birds calm down, the boy paused a moment in spite of his position to glory in the view. The mainland hills stretched blue across the west. Turning east he looked over several islands to the ocean, which he figured stretched away to Spain. Even though his father had assured him the parent herons would not actually attack, the boy continued to scan the sky.

The stench from excrement and rotting fish in the nest was beginning to make the boy feel queasy. He judged it was time to reach up and quickly drop over the crouching chicks the 3-foot-square piece of canvas he had brought.

Flop. Nothing to it. Just like putting a cover on a bird cage. Then he reached his hand under the canvas, into the slimy dark. For an awful moment the boy felt he was going to vomit. Breathing hard, stomach churning, the boy conquered his first heron and triumphantly sent it below. He very quickly acquired the knack for clamping down on a bird, carefully pointing it into a sack, looping shut the mouth of the bag, and lowering it down by rope to the ground.

The younger boy time after time received the precious burden and carried the wriggling bag over to the grassy glade where his father sat. Expertly the biologist removed each bird, tucked its bill under his arm and, with special pliers, fastened a wide, numbered aluminum band on one kicking leg:

AVISE FISH & WILDLIFE SERVICE
WRITE WASHINGTON, DC U.S.A.
807-82050

He spiraled colored bands onto the other leg, recorded several measurements, and returned the bird to the sack to be hoisted up to the nest.

They worked slowly, so there would be no mistakes. It would take all afternoon for one bird after another in the colony to receive its number and the distinctive combination of color bands which would enable the biologist to identify each individual through binoculars in the weeks to come. Soon the birds would be all over the bay, but he would know which birds came from each of the two dozen nests in this rookery.

"Dad, look. I think I found what the trouble was," called the younger boy excitedly. "This was on the ground under that tree over there." The boy held out a young heron nearly dead from exposure and hunger.

"The parents wouldn't go down through all those branches to feed it. They probably wouldn't even recognize it as their own if it was out of the nest. And it couldn't get back up, poor thing. Let's try to warm it up and you can put it back when we finish," said the man as he stuffed the good-sized bird awkwardly inside his shirt to revive it with the heat of his own body.

When the last of the young herons had been measured, weighed, and banded, the man pulled the limp bird from his shirt. The bird responded by vigorously trying to stab.

"Hold on there, rascal," laughed the biologist, who had not been caught unawares. Experience had taught him the peculiar form of gratitude often shown by wild animals he tried to help. Skillfully he immobilized the young heron while he took down its vital statistics and fitted it with bands.

The boy signaled to his brother at the nest at the edge of the rookery. Slowly the squirming bag containing a decidedly revived young heron was pulled up through the branches. In the swaying treetop the boy untied the bundle and carefully placed the young bird back under the canvas in the nest with its siblings.

"There you are, great blue. Better wait till you can fly before you try that again," he murmured.

He eased himself back down from the treetop. When he was half way down the tree, he gave a sharp tug on the cord dangling down from one corner of the canvas square. He held his breath. No herons came tumbling down. He gathered up the canvas and descended, well satisfied with himself.

When the people finally disappeared through the spruces, the anxious mother bird flew to her nest and inspected the youngsters. As the rosy light of sunset faded from the sky, the big heron brought one more fish, which the ravenously hungry adventurer managed to bolt headfirst. The scrawny youngster gulped and snuggled up

14

The young heron hunted in the grassy field.

against the others in the nest, still busy smoothing their rumpled feathers. The bird gave a few pecks at the yellow plastic ring on its right leg and settled into a sound sleep.

The disheveled heron in the outermost nest of the rookery now had a color code—June yellow, right; a number-807-82050; a grand and euphonious scientific name—*Ardea herodias*—and man called him great blue.

On the island across from the herons, the lighthouse sent its warning beams out into the nights. Night and day, the automatic foghorn sounded and was silent, sounded and was silent, over and over again. In the distance a bell buoy gonged faithfully in the swell. The young herons watched distant islands appear and disappear in the coming and going fogs. In the blank whiteness a lobster boat became just voices, radio music, the disembodied drone of an engine.

Sunny noons were enlivened by chattering terns skimming by the island heronry, plunging with a hollow splash after fish. Cormorants whacked the water in great commotion as they ran splashing across the bay in their unique manner of hurling themselves into flight.

On balmy summer nights the herons saw stars twinkle above and double themselves in serene reflections in the great bay. They watched lightning split sultry skies with great claps of thunder. One early July night they listened to a smaller thunder and watched a lightning that was red and yellow and blue and green, as man sent up fireworks that flared, fell, and faded over the harbor of the town across the bay. It was man also who flew the silver birds that whined overhead in the sky, leaving fading tails of white across noon-blue skies, trails that glowed briefly golden in sunsets and vanished.

The tall young heron in the outermost nest watched windjammers under full sail pass by, saw fishing boats heading out to sea, studied man on the lighthouse island. Before darkness fell and the humans disappeared into their tents, they also watched the herons. Concealed by the spruce branches fringing the shore, the biologist and his family could watch through their binoculars the herons returning from all over the bay.

They had enjoyed watching the adult herons on the nest. Gradually they came to identify individual herons by their style of gesture and irregularities in facial plumage, especially the dark spots on the front of their white foreheads.

The herons certainly recognized their mates. The bird on the nest would raise its head alertly as its mate approached. The incoming bird would stretch its neck, erect its crest, and settle in with a low-pitched croaking.

"Arre, arre, arre."

The heron on the nest would greet its mate by standing up and raising its head slowly to the sky in a great stretch. This performance would be elaborated by the bird swaying, neck plumes erected, wrists held out to show off the chestnut lining. A moan like greeting call declared both "I am me" and "I will not attack."

The biologist felt it a special privilege to watch the birds depart in the mornings. As the young herons matured, both parents had to spend the days fishing to feed their young. Sometimes birds flew off in two's, croaking to each other as they flapped off across the bay. Regretfully he acknowledged to himself that this summer's observations were nearly over; the young were almost ready to leave the nest. The island would still be astir in the evenings, but its days would be empty.

One sparkling morning a boy hurried back to his mother who was cooking breakfast on a camp stove perched on a wide pink granite ledge in the sunshine. It was not the smell of food that made the boy run.

"Mom. Dad. Guess what! My heron has fledged. I saw him right in the cove here. He was fishing with another bird. I could see the yellow band on his right leg. I'm so glad he made it."

The boy was right. The adventurous heron had recovered from

his fall. Daily, he had practiced flapping his wings. His flight feathers were fully released from their coverings by hours of careful pecking with his bill. His feathers were properly arranged by days of preening, so that all the minute barbs on the feathers were fastened to each other to make a wing surface both strong and light. The young heron would gain experience in flying—how to land, to handle wind, and the like. Physical maturity and improved coordination of muscles would come to him. Encoded in his genes was information he needed.

The great blue heron simply took off from his nest one day and he flew. He soon followed his father across the short stretch of water to the shallow waters of the little cove. The youngster resembled the older bird except that his breast was blotched and pale; he had only tinges of the rich cinnamon underparts of the adults. He lacked graceful plumes on his back and the pendant black crest of his parents.

He pitched his great wings to brake his descent, and lowered his long legs. For the first time in his life he felt the shock of the cold wetness of the sea. His long, widespread toes distributed his weight over a great enough area on the sand so that the large bird did not sink into the soft bottom.

The tide was fully low. Through the waters that swirled around his legs, great blue's keen eyes could see round green sea urchins on the bottom, even though they had covered themselves with bits of shells to camouflage their spiny selves. Pale-white moon jellyfish came swimming by. Opening and closing their bell-shaped bodies like umbrellas, they moved with a pulsating glide through the water. Clouds of tiny creatures of all kinds-plankton-swirled by.

A school of small silvery fish swam in front of the herons. Deftly the older bird picked up several. The youngster's long bill flashed out like a spear. He missed. He let out a loud "quonk." He stabbed again. He caught one. He stood for a second holding the wriggling fish in his bill, then he tipped back his head. He dropped the fish into the back of his mouth and swallowed it. He watched the older heron catch a fish, and then another. He tried again, and this time he did not miss.

The next day and the day after that, great blue was fishing at dawn in the cove by the lighthouse. He had learned that small green crabs which scuttled about the brown tangles of dripping rockweed were satisfying. Periwinkle snails that crawled slowly over the rocks were not good for him to eat. There was no way he could get at their soft bodies in their brown striped shells. If he poked them or the dog whelks, they merely went in their shells and shut their doors.

On higher and drier rocks he saw a band of white barnacles. These tiny volcanoes housed not a mollusk like the snails, but a curious crustacean that could stand being out of water for a few hours at a time. The tiny creatures lay on their backs inside their cone-shaped shells and waited for the rising tide. When the waves washed over them, they opened the plates at the top and flickered their many legs out into the water to strain out plankton.

At the lower edge of the region exposed by the tides grew short tufts of a reddish-yellow seaweed known as Irish moss. Man sometimes came to rake it off the ledges to make carrageen for thickening salad dressing and ice cream. The rocks in this zone were covered with pink rock crust, an alga that precipitated calcium compounds out of the sea water, and in the crevices were blue mussels fastened firmly to the rocks by dark threads.

In the area only rarely exposed by the lowest tides, where oarweeds and long kelps dangled in deep water, lived the starfish and their relatives, the sea urchins. The great blue did not eat the sea urchins or mussels in their shells even though he saw that the seagulls did. Often as he was fishing, a gull would dart down, seize an urchin or wrench up a mussel, and fly high above the huge pink granite boulders on the shore. The gull would drop the animal, watch its shell break upon the rocks below, and descend to dine upon the soft flesh within the shattered shell.

The young heron wading at the water's edge was unmoved by the plaintive cries of a young gull on the shore behind him. "Eee, eee." The brown-plumaged youngster lowered its head and ran shrieking after a handsome gray-and-white adult bird on the rocks. Time and again the youngster repeated the performance and was ignored—time to learn to fend for itself.

Great blue stood silent and motionless in the sheltered cove. Slowly, so slowly that an observer could scarcely say when the motion began or ceased, he lifted one leg, poised it dripping above the water, and stepped forward again in the water.

A monarch butterfly came skimming over the water. It fluttered by the immobile heron's head, pausing as if to alight. Then it moved on, its bright wings tracing undulations through the sunshine. For all the notice the heron paid the pirouetting insect which shared the cove so intimately, they each might have been inhabiting a separate universe.

A sound which interested the heron very much came to him across the water. Several dozen eider ducklings came paddling, cheeping softly to each other, around the rocky point. All his life the young heron had watched lines of elegant black-and-white male eiders flying low over the water. The circles of warm, soft eiderdown on the bald island just west of the heron rookery were now abandoned. Here were the mothers and babies.

The three drab brown adult females accompanying the little flotilla saw great blue and gave a signal that sent the ducklings paddling urgently away in retreat. If they felt the danger too great, as when a lobster boat was bearing down on them, the young ducklings would simply disappear under water.

The ducklings did appeal to great blue. He might have liked one for dinner. He certainly liked the meadow mice that he found in the grassy field by the lighthouse. Beyond where the blue iris grew he found the tunnels and runways that the mice had bored through the dense grasses. He often heard them squeaking to each other in combat. If he saw one nibbling grass or sampling wild strawberries, he speared with lightning speed. Perhaps the small, dark, furry form would be able to escape in the tunnels of the home range it knew so well, or perhaps great blue would toss it down his throat.

One morning great blue arrived at the cove to be greeted by a furry animal that was decidedly not a mouse. The animal fishing at the water's edge gave a high-pitched, defiant squeal at the great bird. In spite of the razor-sharp teeth that made it a fierce fighter, the mink would have been no match for the heron's powerful beak. Perhaps the mink knew it. Like a flickering shadow the sleek mink retreated to the shelter of an overhanging rock.

Great blue turned his attention to fishing, but already he found the water too deep. Every day the tides advanced by one hour. If great blue intended to fish in the early morning hours, as indeed he did, he would have to look elsewhere for a fishing ground.

He took off, drew back his long neck in the characteristic silhouette of countless generations of great blues before him, and flapped off across the bay.

The great blue heron flew low over the silver water, but as he drew nearer the mainland he altered his flight. Uneasy at all the human activity, he started to climb. He tilted his flapping wings so that more of the under surfaces faced the direction he was flying. Up he rose as more air flowed under his wings than over their smooth curves.

His wing bones were not unlike the bones in a man's arm and hand. The main lift came from his forearm, from what would correspond to his elbow through his wrist. A man would stretch out his arm and bend his hand back at the wrist to imitate the angle of a great blue's wing in flight. The heron used the feathers on the tips of his wings—his hand section—somewhat like propellers. As he flapped along, his wing tips went forward and down, up and back, in countless figure eights.

When he drew up over the land he became aware of a rising column of air. Gliding down the continuously ascending air mass, he rode the warm currents higher and higher. Below him he saw for the first time the endless ocean at the mouth of the bay. Islands beyond number dotted the horizon. Land stretched away to the west as far as he could see. Blue hills with green valleys swept down to the sea. The hilltops seemed to have marched out into the waters to become islands, the valleys between them filled with the sea.

The sun glinted like a flashing mirror on a pond cupped in the dark land below. Young great blue was hungry because he had not fished this morning. The pond looked right to him. Down he dropped even though it did not look or sound like the cove where he had fished before.

All around him great blue heard a deep plunking sound. He saw spreading circles of rippling water and then the yellow throats of calling green frogs. Great blue speared one and ate it. He stepped into the water. The plump form of a tadpole caught his eye. He caught it and ate that too. He raised his head and let a swallow of the sweet water go down his throat. He swallowed more—his first real drink of sweet water.

Great blue flew over to a rock at water's edge to void. It was the way of the herons. After they eat, their bowels move; rarely do they foul the waters where they fish. Only when alarmed do shitepokes earn crude nicknames, leaving the water in a great beating of wings and a trail of white.

In the shallows by the bank was a zone of emergent vegetation, plants which were rooted under the water but reached up to the sunlight: blue-flowering pickerel weed, dainty white arrowhead blossoms among tall cattails. Out where the water was deeper long stems lifted sturdy yellow pond lilies above the surface; round pads of white water lilies floated languidly on the water. Insects crawled in the lily pads, ate the blossoms, ate each other, while still others busily laid eggs on the undersides of the lily pads.

After catching several minnows among the feathery free-floating water weeds, great blue flapped slowly across the still water. In the shade of the far bank five great blue herons were loafing. One was napping with its head tucked down against its back. Several of the others were preening their feathers. The young heron chose a rock for himself and settled down for a nap.

When he awoke, the sun had shifted and the shade had left him. The young great blue felt uncomfortably hot. He held his wings, still folded, out away from his body. Whirligig beetles made circles on the water in front of him. Their eyes were divided so that as they swam along the surface two eyes looked down through the water and two eyes kept watch in the air above. Their doubled vigilance seemed to have paid off: There were a great many beetles swimming there. Ripples of their wake dissipated in a tangle of threadlike vegetation floating on the tepid water. What looked like knots on the threads were tiny bladders—insect traps of the bladderwort.

Swallows swooped occasionally out over the water to pick insects from the air; a white-throated sparrow gave a single whistle; but for the most part the marsh was silent in the sun. The young heron stretched and took off to explore the tea-colored channel that disappeared into the bush at the far end of the pond.

Here the vegetation formed grand and desolate flats punctuated only by an occasional feathery tamarack or the slender spires of black spruces. Like a blanket, mats of sphagnum spread everywhere. Anchored to the triangular stems of sedges poking up from the shallow water, these floating islands of moss supported shrubs—fuzzy-leaved Labrador tea and leatherleaf with tiny, white blossom bells. Arctic plants such as the cotton grass Eskimos used for wicks in their soapstone lamps grew side by side with such southerners as pitcher plants, whose water-filled leaves trapped and digested

23

unwary insects. Tiny spoon-shaped leaves covered with sticky red hairs—the sundews—nestled down among the sphagnum and waited for smaller insects to blunder into them. The waters of this shallow saucer scooped out of the granite island were very poor in calcium and basic salts. Insectivorous plants, which were adapted to such conditions, had a competitive advantage over the other plants: They carried on photosynthesis as the others did, but they were able to supplement their diets with insects.

As the heron walked across the boggy floating carpet, the vegetation trembled; delicate pink-fringed orchids nodded to him. Finding little to eat, the heron flew back across the still flats to the open marsh. As he dropped down among the cattails, a mother black duck hurried her thirteen ducklings away. A large dark shadow appeared in the water; the sinister, pointed snout of a snapping turtle faced the wading bird.

The big old turtle silently submerged and glided purposefully toward him. Great blue took a step back. The turtle swerved; a fluffy duckling paddled furiously across the water. The hungry snapping turtle pulled it under by one little black leg. Powerless to defend the rest of her young ones, the mother black duck frantically urged them on. Great blue saw the awesome power in those jaws and took to the air.

The Indian boy narrowed his dark eyes as he fixed them on his prey, the tall heron before him. Soundlessly as he could, he inched forward on his stomach through the marsh grasses. A crab scuttled away. The boy grimaced as his knee passed over a sharp barnacle-covered rock. Slowly, slowly he narrowed the distance between them.

The great blue spied the movement in the grasses and, with an indignant squawk, took off. The boy sat up and watched with awe the beating of the great sky-colored wings. Then he laughed and sent a whoop of his own private meaning ringing after the bird.

Under his mother's frown he returned to the task that brought him to the salt marsh: gathering sweet grass. The Indian family had come from their ancestral island up the Penobscot River. They came in a pickup truck. They came to enjoy the seashore and to gather a special seaside grass of lasting fragrance for making baskets. They called it sweet grass and wove it onto splints of ash wood.

Thousands of herons had been stalked by Penobscot boys over the years. Shell heaps on the bank behind the boy lay several yards thick. The Ancients, as the Penobscots called their forebears, had paddled down from their winter lodges at the head of the Penobscot River to summer here on the islands. Clay pots, handsome harpoons carved of bone, flint arrowheads, and the like, lay in the shell heaps, discarded as long as four thousand years ago. In canoes made of birch bark sewn with spruce roots and caulked with spruce gum, the Ancients came. They dug clams, caught fish and herons, ate berries, and grew fat. By drying and smoking, they put up what they could for the long winter ahead.

The boy was delighted when at last his mother released him from the chore of picking sweet grass stem by stem. The tide had gone out far enough to expose the clam flats. Gathering clams was a chore much more to his liking. He exchanged his meager bundle of grass for a clam roller—a cradle-shaped basket of wooden slats—took up a clam rake, and slogged off across the flats to dig clams.

The great blue heron moved to the far side of the cove, complaining loudly as he flew. These flats were favored fishing grounds for many herons. The stream at the head of the cove washed down nutrients from the land. The flats provided a vital nursery ground for the tender pollution-sensitive stages of many creatures of the sea. Herons were able to hunt profitably for several hours on both the rising and falling tides as fish came in from deeper waters to feed on the abundance of life in the salt marsh.

Where the water was still lapping lived sand dollars whose fuzzy green covering nearly concealed the five-rayed pattern they shared with the starfish and sea urchins. Razor clams nearly six inches long lived buried upright in the water-covered mud, siphoning in water from which they filtered out food, passing the water back out. Although the elusive razor clams were delicious eating, the Indian boy was not even going to try to capture them. He wanted littleneck clams, so he had chosen a spot where the tides had left the flats bare, where softly rounded hillocks of mud were peppered with holes the diameter of a drinking straw. He put his clam roller gently down beside him and bent from the waist in a straddling stance.

Slock!

The tines of his clam rake whacked into the sucking mud. One hand gave a prying motion to the rake while the other darted into the opened chasm to pluck clams out of the black claylike mud. He grabbed two gray-blue clams and tossed them into his roller. Two escaped. A jet of water from the siphon of a retreating clam squirted his head.

"Piss clam!" chortled the boy as he wiped his forehead on the rolled up sleeve of his faded flannel shirt.

He was just straightening up after a spell of digging when a wriggling movement caught his attention. His muddy fingers pulled a foot-long greenish clam worm out of its hole. The boy studied its fringe of external gills a moment as it writhed on his palm. Then he coiled it up and shoved it into his pocket, thinking he might go fishing later.

The mud of the drier zone behind him was crisscrossed with the tracings of mud snails—a periwinkle which had evolved lungs—and hermit crabs. These borrowers grew no shell of their own, but backed their abdomen into empty periwinkle shells. When they outgrew one home they simply moved on to a larger shell, trading whelk shells for moon snail shells.

The plants grew in ranks along the shore according to their

ability to withstand salt or submersion: bayberry and rugosa rose at the back of the beach by the Indians' truck, then salt hay and sea oats where two black-eyed girls were playing house with sea shells, and finally eelgrass growing well beyond the clammers, under water all but a few hours of the day. Eelgrass was one of the few flowering plants to invade the ocean—nearly all the other seaweeds were much simpler algae. Satiny green ribbons of eelgrass sheltered the little fish that fed the great blue herons.

The water ahead of great blue suddenly frothed and flashed, as a school of herring darted between his legs. A school of silvery-blue mackerel gobbled up the herring in the rear while the heron caught them in front. He speared a good-sized mackerel as it darted past. The heron held the large fish aloft a moment and then took it over and laid it on a flat rock. He stabbed a few times at the fish's gill area. The gleaming iridescent striped mackerel gave a convulsive twitch and flopped back into the water. Giving a splash, it darted away, leaving the young heron staring at the empty rock.

The Indian boy across the flats stood grinning with a muddy face.

Day by day the hours of sunlight shortened—by the length of a bird's foot, the Penobscots said. With blueberry rakes—baskets bearing comblike tines which stripped the berries from the bushes—the Indians had harvested miles and miles of blueberry barrens down east. The moon of the ripe berries gave way to the moon of fat seals and red leaves.

The young great blue herons that were dispersed northward along the Maine coast had been joined by flocks of ruddy turnstones, whose patterned backs exactly matched the dark brown seaweeds on the red rocks. Black-bellied plovers and several kinds of sandpipers appeared on the clam flats. They had all come south from the Arctic. Having built their nests and raised their young far above the Arctic Circle, they were already on their way to spend the winter at the other end of the world.

The sea, too, was showing the change of seasons. The bay danced with whitecaps on sparkling clear, breezy, blue September days. Rocks bore empty shells of mussels and barnacles as the season of plenty drew to a close. The large fish of the sea were moving in schools to deeper waters where the temperatures would remain more constant during the long, cold winter ahead.

Ashore the human race, many of them, also embarked on a fall migration: Summer people went back to the cities. The harbors once again belonged to the fishing boats, the streets in the little villages to the year-round residents. The tiny warblers from the islands had all donned their subdued fall plumage and flown south. The monarch butterflies had made their fragile but relentless way down the coast to Mexico.

The young herons of the bay grew restless. Their bodies were strong and firm, plump with reserves of fat stored under their skin. One night the stars seemed to glitter nearer than ever before. The temperature dropped. The first cold glints of morning sparkled on frost. Frost covered the fields, the rooftops, the boats turned bottomside-up in backyards. Frost gilded the hedges and wharfs, and even the seaweeds on the rocks. The young herons were gone. Singly and in small flocks they had flown. In a few days or weeks the older birds would follow. This year's crop of herons would find the way for themselves. But only one or two of every four of them would live to return.

Great blue headed out to sea. Harbor seals lying on a rock ledge eyed him impassively as he flew. Seals of all ages were lying in bizarre poses on the bare ledge not yet claimed by the rising tide. Their silky coats gleamed in the early morning sunlight. They were sleek yet fat, all shades of pearly gray, some nearly rust colored, hoary elders and spotted pups. Pulling with their flippers, several seals humped awkwardly over the rocks. At the water's edge they poured themselves gracefully in. Here was the element to which they were adapted. They closed their slitlike nostrils and submerged. The cold depths of water bothered them not at all, wrapped as they were in a protective coat of blubber just under their skin. Their bobbing heads rising from the sea to look curiously around briefly resembled lobster-pot buoys. Then they vanished.

The rising sun seemed to catch the bay still sleeping in glassy stillness. As silently as a painted crane on a silken Chinese scroll, the young great blue heron winged out over the calm water.

A percussive "chuff" exploded out of the water beneath the heron—a porpoise exhaling. Five times in quick succession the sound came—like a human coughing into a length of pipe—as all the members of the group surfaced, breathed, and sank.

For a time the porpoises circled at the surface, perhaps feeding. Then they moved off together, one young porpoise swimming so close to its mother and copying the timing of her breathing so exactly that an observer from shore would believe them to be one. The five porpoises surfaced in sequence just a scant second after one another. Their smooth dark backs gleamed, arched, and disappeared in their own mystic rhythm, again and again.

When the young heron left the small islands of the bay behind, he began to meet pelagic birds. Welcoming him to this new realm were small dark petrels skimming lightly over the wave tops. A greater shearwater rode the air currents inches above the water. Its very long wings bore the gull-sized body of the shearwater along in a nearly uninterrupted glide. A small clownish puffin beat by, tiny wings buzzing, bright red feet dangling. It nosed its gay parrotlike bill into the freshening breeze, the jester announcing the lord of the realm.

As if some magic mischievous child were playing out here with a garden hose, a column of water rose suddenly before the heron.

29

It was vapor, the color of the pearly lining inside a mussel shell—the blow of a whale. A finback, second largest of all the great whales, appeared at the surface. Its long forehead submerged while its back continued to come into view: the graceful dark sickle of a fin, exquisite living line of the back, more and more whale curving into the sunlight—perhaps thirty feet at a time, but nearly twice that much unrevealed. With a swirl of flukes the whale sounded. An oily slick calmed the water like a footprint where the majestic finback had been but a moment before.

Spout. Spout. Spout. The whale moved on its way. As the young heron continued south across the Gulf of Maine, crossing the cold currents flowing down from the north, he met other whales on their migrations. Sei and finback whales which had spent the summer straining countless tons of plankton from Arctic waters were passing down the coast. Now and then the pear-shaped blow of a humpback whale appeared in the distance; black fins of small pilot whales would appear and disappear in synchrony.

Below great blue stretched the Georges Banks, drowned when the glaciers melted, once famous for their inexhaustible supplies of cod, haddock, and that staple of the sea's food web, the herring. No great shoals of herring did the heron see spawning there.

On and on flew the great blue heron. Miles of empty ocean faded into the distance behind him. Never really empty, the ocean had life spread thinly through it, and trash, flotsam of man's civilization. A deep-blue band marked the warm flow of the Gulf Stream. Making good speed with the help of a tail wind, the heron was able to cruise at an altitude of six thousand feet. Beneath him sped flocks of ducks also making their way south, and occasionally he met other herons and a few egrets.

The small, dark petrals skimmed lightly over the wave tops.

The heron lacked the complete waterproofing of the ducks. Landing on the open ocean for a rest was for the large bird a possible but dangerous proposition at best. The array of floating objects below seemed to be mostly bits of plastic refuse, none of it large enough to guarantee a safe, dry landing, or more important, a take-off. Nearly eighteen hours ago the land had disappeared behind him. To the west lay North America, some five hundred miles away. To the east lay Europe, four times that far. South, ever southward flew the great blue.

At last before him on the horizon his eyes picked out a welcoming sight, and the wind carried a welcoming fragrance—land.

2
BERMUDA

THE YOUNG HERON SAW below him clearer waters than ever he had encountered before, a dazzling expanse of aquamarine. Dark patches in many shades of lavender and green marked the living coral reefs of Sea Venture Flats, which men named for the first ships which wrecked there. Beyond lay the chain of islands called Bermuda. Fifteen miles long, two miles wide, and five hundred eighty-eight miles due east of North Carolina, the islands of Bermuda are the top of an extinct volcano. Seas covered the summit of this ancient mountain as the Ice Age glaciers melted, and on its top corals grew abundantly in the sunny waters—as far north as corals are able to grow anywhere on earth. Not once, but several times, the waters subsided, the wind eroded the reefs to sand, and blew dunes into shape. Turned by time into rock, the hills of Bermuda came thus into being.

On the dark and gentle contours loomed a huge pink hotel towering above the town of St. George, dwarfing like a toy the ramparts of Fort St. Catherine which had guarded the island in the Victorian era when Bermuda was Britain's "Gibraltar of the Western Hemisphere." Those days were past, and tourism was now the fiber of Bermuda's being.

The great blue heron winged his way over the quaint town. Like steps, thin blocks of limestone were set in whitewashed courses up the roofs to gather precious rain water, for Bermuda's porous limestone, sitting like a sponge in the world's saltiest ocean, is not suitable for wells.

With mild interest, a tourist standing by the recreated wooden stocks in the old town square noted the big bird flying slowly overhead. Great blue herons here, just like back home.

Great blue headed out across St. George's harbor, over the waterfront with its replica of the ship the *Sea Venture* castaways built to carry them on to Virginia, over the sleek dark forms of two U.S. Navy submarines tied up alongside the little wooden ship, out across the mammoth airfield created from scores of small islets in Castle Harbor. After World War II it was opened to civilian flights, and birds of a different feather began flocking to Bermuda. The jumbo jet which was just then disgorging several hundred tourists loomed nearly as large as a terminal building.

Great blue noticed one larger island before him in Castle Harbor that was unlike any of the others; it was clothed almost entirely in green. He flew to it. Nonsuch Island sanctuary. The heron landed on the pale gold beach. The sand was powder soft, still radiating heat from the afternoon sun. Great blue waded out into the water. Warm! He caught himself a dinner. The fish were strange to him— small, yellow-and-black brightly striped mouthfuls. Abudefdufs, or sergeant majors, they were, and great blue found them good.

The sun dropped behind the mainland and lights twinkled across the low dark hills as the heron walked up the beach, superimposing his large footprints on the tracks of turnstones and sanderlings, as well as on the strange, gracefully rhythmic tracings of the Bermuda skink, a small lizard found nowhere in the world but Bermuda. Great blue flew to a gnarled, silvery, dead cedar tree and prepared to spend the night in its shelter, safe on Nonsuch Island.

In the middle of the night a strange wailing sound awakened the great blue. The wind was light and waves gently lapped the shore. In the middle distance a fringe of moon-painted waves was breaking on Gurnet Rock, but the sea was not moaning.

The bobbing light of a flashlight came moving along the dark path between the palmettos. As the heron tensed, the footsteps crunching along the path turned abruptly. The human picked its way through the rocks to the south beach.

For nearly an hour the island seemed to hold its breath as the human betrayed its presence on the beach by small rattlings in the dark and the piercing arc of its light.

Once again the footsteps approached the vigilant heron, but passed without pausing. Once again the gentle lapping of the waves.

"Oooh-eek, ooooo-eek!"

Eerie cries sounded in the darkness not far away.

"Oooh-eek."

Dawn shed little light on the source of the strange cries that had disturbed the heron's sleep. Huge pleated fans of palmetto leaves rustled in the breezes. Several times in the night great blue had been fooled by the clicking sound they made. He had heard raindrops but none fell from the sky.

The morning sun highlighted on the other end of the island a large, once-elegant house. Great blue listened intently as someone left the house and came striding energetically down through the trees to the shore. He watched with interest as a sandy haired, bearded man in ragged shorts jumped nimbly into a boat and headed off across the channel.

The man was David Wingate. With even greater interest he had watched great blue arrive in Bermuda. Through the powerful telescope mounted in the dish of the radar installation on Cooper's Island, he had seen a heron when it was nearly fifteen miles out of Bermuda. Flying at about three thousand feet, the great blue was picked up by radar. Wingate, who could see the color of the heron's eye and the bands on its legs, identified the incoming bird using the telescope. He had been invited to use the NASA equipment built for tracking the lunar spacecrafts of the Apollo projects. With visiting scientists he was identifying migrating birds, correlating the telescopic observations with the radar information to help men learn more about the annual flights of the birds. Other observers on ships at sea were gathering similar data.

Small, quickly moving images appearing on their radar screens told them that shorebirds were passing by; large slow-moving "angels" as they called the radar blips indicated the herons which had been passing all this week, and small erratic images that appeared and disappeared told them that groups of warblers were arriving. Most New England birds were migrating along the east coast of the mainland, but those which ventured out over the ocean would face practically no predators and they would find the overwater trip to the Caribbean shorter than the Florida route by nearly half. By far the greater portion of these transoceanic adventurers did not even stop to rest on Bermuda, but the radar patterns seemed to indicate that birds were stopping on Bermuda yesterday.

Wingate knew that a hurricane was reported brewing down in the Caribbean, but how could the birds know that? For that matter, how did they find Bermuda in the first place? Birds seemed to be navigating by the sun, but how do they manage when it's cloudy? To what extent do they use the stars, or some innate inherited map, or something man does not sense, like electromagnetic fields? The scientists were getting closer, but for the time being it remained the herons' secret.

The great blue heron loafing on the shore of Nonsuch watched Wingate's boat disappear behind the next island and then spent the morning exploring. He fished a bit along the shore of wind-carved limestone, gray rocks horizontally banded, layer upon layer, eroded into countless pinnacles, knife sharp and paper thin. Silvery twisted branches of the shrub Bermudians call sea lavender framed a striking panorama of rugged gray islets in a bright ultramarine sea. White birds with foot-long streamer tails flew back and forth before the island cliffs: white-tailed tropicbirds, the longtails. Soon they would head out to sea for the winter. A pair of the graceful longtails flew by, one above the other, their wings beating in unison, the tips of their long tail feathers touching.

The young heron dozed in the shade of bay grapes, tall shrubs with saucerlike leaves. Goldfinches—the European kind with decorative gold wing bars and red face patches—plucked seeds from sea oxeye, a few blooms still showing yellow at the edge of the rocks. Everywhere the sandy ground was pockmarked with the burrows of land crabs. Bright flame-orange Gulf fritillary butterflies flashed through the noon sunshine visiting small passion flowers on their trailing vines.

The sound of a boat's motor interrupted the heron's nap. It was Wingate returning, but this time he did not land on great blue's island. His sturdy boat pounded out across the waves to the tiny islets off Nonsuch. The wind had risen and was lashing the seas

37

to shining emerald waves. A gathering swell which threatened to engulf the boat from behind plunged swiftly, silently, beneath the little craft and carried it high into the air. The boat came down to meet the sea with a resounding smack. Wingate smiled into the wind and spread his stance more firmly to keep his balance.

David Wingate was Bermuda's chief conservation officer. Nonsuch as a living museum of primeval Bermuda flora and fauna was his creation. Almost single-handedly he had rooted out alien species of plants and replaced them with native plants—thousands and thousands of seedlings over the years, but an even more challenging task awaited him on the small islands, for they were the home of the cahows, the only remaining Bermuda petrels in the world, some of the rarest birds in the world, some hundred breeding birds. If the weather gave him any chance at all, Wingate would carefully check lonely islets; it was time for the annual return of the cahows.

The end of Nonsuch Island claimed by the sojourning heron narrowed in such a way that the north-facing beach was nearly back to back with its south-facing twin. To the hunting heron an hour on the northern side of the island passed almost with haste. In due course he ventured over to the south side where he discovered a wire enclosure at the back of the beach. Emerging from it was a line of tiny toylike green turtles. Hatchlings scrambled down the beach and straight out to sea as fast as their little flippers could carry them. The baby turtles left miniature furrows behind them in the damp sand. A number of these tracks disappeared abruptly, well above the water line. On tall stilt legs, the great blue heron seesawed his long neck down and scooped up the turtles one after another. The heron found them tender and tasty.

A shout resounded from the palmettos behind him. Startled, great blue took to the air. Wingate appeared waving his arms and shouting after the departing heron. The hatchlings were part of the international Operation Green Turtle, an expensive snack for visiting herons. Several thousand green sea turtle eggs from Costa

Rica had been flown to Bermuda where Wingate had buried them in the sand on the protected beach at Nonsuch. Once native to Bermuda, green turtles had long ago been eliminated from Bermuda's waters by overhunting. The fact that they were also disappearing throughout the Caribbean prompted the restocking project. It was hoped that the young turtles would imprint the location where they hatched upon their memories and return to these same beaches to lay their eggs. They would be less vulnerable to man's encroachment if all their eggs were not in one basket, the one beach in Costa Rica.

Day after day Wingate had checked the white eggs buried in the sand, incubated by the end-of-summer sun. Finally, last night the hatchlings in a group effort had struggled to the surface where they were met by Wingate. By fastening miniature sonar tracking devices of neutral buoyancy to the carapaces of the baby turtles, he hoped to help solve the mystery of where green turtles go for the first year of their lives. These little live messages-in-a-bottle carried out to sea might give man a clue to protecting them.

Wingate thought he had tagged and released from the safety of the wire enclosure all of this year's hatch. So he thought, but some of the turtles had remained in the artificial nest, perhaps trapped by collapsing sand. At any rate, last night in the dark Wingate had overlooked them, but this morning the great blue heron had not.

Wingate scowled at the tracks in the sand and stamped his foot. Sand trickled in through the holes in his sneaker. He sat down heavily beside the enclosure. Seeing a plant not native to Bermuda, he automatically pulled it up. His anger slowly burned away, not to ashes of despair but to disappointment, which is all the truly dedicated allow themselves in the face of setbacks.

Can't win 'em all. The whole world is waiting out there to eat those little turtles.

Across the glowing turquoise waters beckoned Bermuda, the land to which Wingate had given nearly all the years of his life. That bright confetti of houses—there were so many of them now.

Bermuda had become the most densely populated island in the world. His gaze ranged out to sea where he had recently been spending as much time as he could in a small boat studying pelagic birds. He treasured what peace and renewal he found out there, for he knew there would never be enough money, enough manpower, enough time for the job he had chosen.

He rose and began to dismantle the turtle pen, turning over in his mind several projects which would put the wire to good use.

As the man did not show any signs of leaving the beach, the young heron flew over to one of the islets just off the end of Nonsuch. Here he fished, and found himself a sheltered roost on a rocky ledge. As he was drawing his head in, his eye caught a movement in the grass. It was the first of the land crabs emerging from its hole for its evening foraging. As the crab scuttled sideways along its usual pathway, the heron scooped it up. He stood motionless for a few minutes and was able to grab up another, and another, and another. Wingate would have appreciated that. He struggled to keep the land crab population in check while the ground cover of small native plants was reestablishing itself.

With a full stomach, great blue went to sleep that night, but once again eerie wailings interrupted his slumbers. He peered out into the darkness.

"Ooh, ow, cahow." Cahows crying their own name. They had returned to Bermuda. In a part of their breeding ritual they were landing at the mouth of their cliffside burrows. Then they took off again into the night air, wailing and flying about and landing, again and again. The adults had come to lay and brood their single egg over the winter and feed their solitary chick in the spring. They would fish at sea by day, returning only at night. When the young cahow was ready to fledge, it would fly off to sea, reappearing two years later to raise young of its own on the tiny islets off Bermuda. Remarkable tubelike organs on their nostrils desalt drinking water for these oceanic petrels; their diet is fish; more chicks are successfully hatching now that North American use of DDT has declined, but where they go in all the wide seas, no man really knows. The great blue heron could just discern their dark forms fluttering in the moonlight.

Great blue stirred uneasily and awoke. The air was uncomfortably hot and heavy yet the sun was barely up. A haze hung in the sky—dust borne on the winds from drought-stricken Africa where men had traded rainforest for desert. But it was more than that. The sea was as still as glass and wore a peculiar leaden sheen. The young heron was restless, and yet somehow it did not feel to him like the right sort of day for continuing his journey south.

He lifted off from the rocky islet and, in compromise, flew across to the mainland. From the height, the heron could see from one end to the other of the long narrow fishhook shape that was Bermuda. He could see the concentration of buildings that was Hamilton, the capital city; Hamilton, where the cruise ships docked. Taller than the glittering shops along Front Street loomed the great ships.

The heron looked down upon large hotels set in the midst of rolling, carefully manicured grounds marked with the distinctive patterns of golf course greens and sand traps. Rows and rows of white roofs glimmered on the hillsides, their walls bright with pastel colors, the gardens hedged with red hibiscus and pink oleander. A profusion of many-colored blooms drooped languidly in the end-of-summer heat.

The beaches shimmered pink in the sun. Narrow roads designed for horse and buggy twisted in and out through high-walled cuts in gray hills. Motorbikes buzzed like flies in the sticky heat. Automobiles blurred by; lines of taxis loaded high with luggage, and ponderous pink buses made their way along the shore road.

41

In a valley between the busy road and the glassy sea, great blue found sanctuary at Spittal Pond, a sixty-acre natural treasure. The tracks of hundreds of shorebirds crisscrossed the mud flats at water's edge. For the last month, shorebirds from the Arctic had been streaming over Bermuda on a direct route, straight south from Newfoundland, down to South America.

The great blue eyed a large gathering of mallards and blue-winged teal dabbling in the shallow water remaining in the center of the pond after the long dryness of summer. They were dining royally in huge mats of yellowish algae. The heron stepped to the pond shore. The soupy warm waters teemed with gambusia, the tiny mosquito minnows brought to Bermuda in 1942 in an early and successful attempt at biological control of Yellow Fever-carrying mosquitoes. The heron snapped them up right and left and tossed the little fish down his throat with the animated singlemindedness of a giant mechanical wind-up toy.

Bermuda has not always been so fortunate in the plant and animal species introduced to her shores. An accidentally introduced scale insect denuded the entire island of its tree cover of native Bermuda cedars. The young heron retired to the shade of some of the shaggy pinelike casuarina trees which had been brought from Australia to replace the cedars.

From the treetops a bright yellow-bellied, black-masked bird was lustily calling its own name: kis-ka-dee, kis-ka-dee, imported to prey on lizards which had been brought in earlier. A handful of chirping house sparrows sifted down from the trees to patrol the path for crumbs of contraband cookies dropped by passing school groups. The noisy squabbling of a flock of starlings was the only other bird sound in the noontime stillness.

The dozing heron woke to full alertness as some humans came strolling though the park on their lunch hour. A single Bermuda bluebird, hard put to maintain its existence in the face of competition from these immigrant species, flitted through the lichen-draped branches above the heron.

Tiny warblers, first time voyagers like the young great blue heron, twitted softly to each other in the shadows. The yellow-rumped warblers, black-throated greens, and parulas hopped about uneasily, picking occasional insects from the branches, refueling before they too headed farther south.

As the great blue heron roused himself, a flash of movement drew his attention: a pair of Jamaica anoles. The smaller lizard was a soft gray, barred in a black-and-white pattern down her back. She darted down from the dead branch where she had been sunning to scoop up a small black beetle. Methodically she chewed it until she could swallow it with a gulp.

The larger lizard, a male, was colored quite differently: green with a lavender-blue tail. He saw the heron. Perhaps anxiously, perhaps defiantly, he bobbed his head up and down. He thrust out

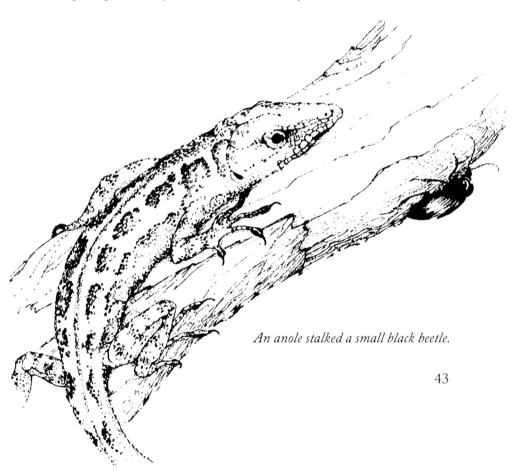

An anole stalked a small black beetle.

43

a bright orange throat sac. Fortunately for him, the great blue's attention was elsewhere. Unfortunately for the little gray female, great blue had been watching her. He snapped her up. Great blue turned and lunged for the male. The anole dashed away leaving his still-wriggling tail in the mouth of the young heron. The lizard forfeited his lovely lavender-blue tail for his life—a good exchange, as he would in time grow another tail.

Although the great blue heron could still see heat waves shimmering in the air in front of the layered cliffs, his restlessness eventually drove him to abandon the shade. He flew out into the sunlight. Even the sandy crabgrass felt hot to great blue's feet. The tall heron bent down his long neck to peer into the dark of a large land crab hole. A huge gold-and-purple eye peered back. From under horny, knobbed eyebrows, a grapefruit-sized toad regarded the heron. Warty and inscrutable, the giant toad rested in the relative cool and safety of its borrowed burrow.

The rocks along the shore felt even hotter to the great blue's feet. He walked carefully around a large pool of tar bubbling in the heat. The black ooze had collected behind a cut in the rocks where the sea washed in. Tankers were wont to dump their ballasts and wastes, flush their bilges, at sea. The resulting tar floated ashore in great fistfuls to be cursed by bathers where the noxious blobs marred the beaches.

Inspection of a tide pool acquainted great blue with dark, mottled crabs scurrying off to safety. As in Maine, periwinkle snails grazed on the dark haze of microscopic blue-green algae, but here they were slender striped zebra periwinkles. Another black-and-white snail frequented the little pools scoured out of the aeolian limestone—the baby tooth shells. An empty baby tooth clearly showed two tiny white "teeth" along the edge of its shell. Huge chitons several inches long, simple mollusks covered with eight plates of shell fitted together like armor, clung to the wet rocks, safe from the big bird.

The heron had become aware that the sea was no longer calm. Great long swells were breaking over the offshore reefs. Up on the hillside men were hammering fast shutters on their homes. In the harbors they were moving their boats to safer anchorages. Anxiously men watched their barometers and listened to the weather reports which informed them of the progress of a hurricane headed toward Bermuda.

With morning came the rain. A downpour sent the great blue to the shelter of a small cave eroded out of the limestone layers. Towers of dark clouds piled up over Bermuda. Rain pelted down. Winds piled up huge seas before them; waves thundered on the reefs and hurled themselves against the cliffs, shattering to the sky.

Shrieking winds out of the northeast stripped the bay grape at the door of great blue's cave of its leaves. The trees, casuarinas and cedars alike, writhed, rubbed, scraped against each other in the agony of the storm, and broke. The bole of an entire palmetto came hurtling through the air like a javelin.

At a hundred miles an hour, the great counter-clockwise wheel of hurricane winds beat Bermuda. Power lines snapped like rubber bands. Roofing slates and man's forgotten belongings sailed through the air to unlikely resting places.

Suddenly the storm stopped. The air seemed bewitched in eerie, unearthly silence. The pressure dropped; men huddling in their houses watched their barometers plunge to nine-tenths of what the air pressure registered normally. The eye of the storm was upon Bermuda, looking for uncautious fools to venture out. The hub of the wheel of winds took just half an hour to pass by the great blue heron and Bermuda.

Great blue, like all of his kind, was not what men would call impatient. He was standing immobile, safe in the cave in the hillside at Spittal Pond Sanctuary, like a garden statue in storage, when the winds struck again. This time the winds bore down from the southwest. They raged even more furiously than before. Waves dashed spume forty, fifty, eighty feet up into the air. Inescapable salt spray stung in the air. The banana crop was ruined; the blossoms of the island were gone; leaves were lashed from all the vegetation.

45

Water poured in over the cuts and low places between the rocks. The sea had come to join Spittal Pond. The ponds of the refuge were no longer surrounded by parched, cracked mud flats baked by the sun; they had become subsets of the sea.

The rains began to let up. The winds roared less loudly. Tentatively, the sun peered through the clouds. Great blue, and indeed everything that was lucky enough to be still alive, felt in the air a new freshness, an inviting coolness. In Bermuda, too, summer was over.

Most of the hurricanes born in the Caribbean vent their fury on the West Indies or the Gulf Coast and southern United States. Windy Bermuda only occasionally bears the full brunt of a tropical storm. Nevertheless, *Ya de Demonios,* Isles of Devils, the Spaniards had called the Bermudas. More than one of His Majesty's ships laden with Inca gold from the Spanish Main had wrestled here with the devils and lost. The bones of ships and men lay among the reefs where the waves were boiling.

The tiny fish mimicked the Sargasso weed.

3

The Sargasso Sea

THE HERON FLEW WITH little effort over the sea pulsing uneasily below him. Southward the great bird went, taking advantage of the windy, clear weather of the high pressure system that had moved in after the storm.

The birds—warblers, thrushes, shorebirds, all that had paused on Bermuda—left behind a quite different assortment of birds at Spittal Pond. The Bermuda Islands had attracted windblown strays like a magnet. The brimming, brackish waters of the flooded sanctuary welcomed from Europe a whimbrel, a dappled brown shorebird with a distinctive decurved bill. The migrants left a lone pink flamingo hungrily scooping organisms from the mud. Caught by the strong winds of the north-racing hurricane, the flamingo was separated from its flock, its fate no longer linked with that of the others which may have perished at sea or returned safely to their communal grounds in the brine lakes of Great Inagua Island in the Bahamas. The flamingo had traveled hundreds of miles north in the grip of the storm. That far south and even farther headed flock after flock of avian travelers with the fine weather.

The great blue heron heading out over the coral flats well before dawn could occasionally hear the snapping of shrimp, the sounds the fish made to each other, sounds produced by the swim bladder, or grinding teeth perhaps. He watched bottle-nosed dolphins leap from the water in unison. Their glove-soft skin gleamed pearly-gray in the moonlight as their curving bodies cleaved the air. Because the interface between air and water transmits sound so poorly, the great blue heard only the smallest fraction of the phonations the dolphins naturally use for communication, not the squeaking, bubbling, buzzing sounds they have been trained to produce in shows. When the great dark shape of a humpback whale passed beneath the soaring bird, little of the moaning, trumpeting, and whistling of its songs reached the heron's ears. Sometimes the humpbacks would breach close to the heron. A great leviathan would hurl itself out of the water, pause as if defying gravity, and fall back into the sea with a magnificent curling splash, its long white flippers trailing streamers of foam. Another whale, perhaps two miles away, would simultaneously enact the performance, indicating that the two had somehow been in communication with each other. The whales, too, were heading south where they would have their calves in the sunny equatorial waters.

Now and again in the early morning stillness the heron would hear the coughing of a great turtle as it pushed its horny, beaked snout above the surface; it exhaled in a rush of bubbles, silently breathed in, and submerged once more, foreflippers paddling slowly in unison, carrying the big turtle down under water, out of sight. A swirl of bubbles and a trail of excrement marked the turtle's path. Tiny fish appeared from nowhere and snapped up the bits of undigested food in the excrement. The shells of hawksbill turtles had all too often journeyed these waters in days gone by as artistically wrought tortoiseshell objects, stashed with jewels, silks, and gold and silver in the ships of Bermuda privateers.

The rising sun picked out, on the western horizon, oil tankers and ore carriers from South America riding the Gulf Stream, that river of warm water, bigger than the mighty Mississippi, flowing through the ocean at three miles an hour.

Whitecaps marked the sea surface in neat white lines of scalloped edging, ranked evenly as far as the eye could see: scales on a fish, a mythologically giant fish, the monster Sargasso Sea. When Columbus sailed the Sargasso Sea, his men, checking it for rocks and reefs, found it unusually deep, unusually salty and warm. Soon sailors were warning each other away from this forbidding lair of sea monsters, where a ship would surely get becalmed, trapped in the clutches of miles and miles of seaweed, to become one more ghost ship manned by a crew of skeletons doomed to the dread Sargasso forever.

A yacht, height-dwarfed, her sails gleaming scimitars, heeled gracefully far below the heron. A few small clouds cast purple shadows on the sea as great blue winged steadily over the giant seaweed-strewn oval a thousand miles wide and two thousand miles long, virtually without current, the unmoving hub of a giant wheel. Heated by the direct rays of the tropical sun, the warm, still waters of the hub of this gyre expanded, raising the level of the Sargasso Sea over which the young heron passed some four feet higher than the level of the sea at the American coast.

Far below the heron a unique community was carrying on its own existence. Barnacles, crabs, and shrimp with special adaptations for spending their whole lives aboard the floating mats of brown algae made the Sargasso Sea their home. A perfectly camouflaged little fish with mottled brown fins trailing like tatters of seaweed flitted into hiding. No creatures achieved very great numbers in the unusually clear, nutrient-poor water. A lone tropicbird from time to time would come skimming by, gliding in effortless grace just above the waves.

The great blue heron flew high over the glittering ocean. He flew high enough to avoid the strong currents of southeast trade winds, where the thin, cold air offered only half as much oxygen as it did at sea level. Since his lungs were beautifully adapted with a countercurrent flow of blood and air, he winged smoothly through the vast arc of the sky, deepest blue at its zenith overhead.

The heron flew through sunset, through night, through dawn, and into another day with only the ocean, an osprey, a small flock of warblers and an occasional string of southbound blue-wing teal for company.

Some forty-eight hours after the migrants left Bermuda, they approached Antigua. They were joined by others of their species who had come down the coast of the continent and were making their way along the islands which ring the Caribbean Sea.

Those which had braved the ocean shortcut did not halt as land came into view. Quite the contrary: Great blue and the others increased their altitude and continued down the emerald island chain of the Lesser Antilles. Green volcanic cones, steep and young, marked the Windward Islands of the Antilles group, peaks shrouded in clouds, every one.

Late in the afternoon great blue began to lose altitude. Flat sheets of woolly clouds became ugly, gray, swirling, seething banks. To fly within such a cloud was to be eclipsed. Surrounded by vaporous gray, buffeted by invisible currents, unable to see the swallowing sea beneath, the heron fought its way back up above the clouds. A mammoth jet appeared with unearthly suddenness in an opening between the cloud banks. A shaft of sunlight caught its huge silver wings. Exploding in a dazzling corona, the strange brilliance passed over the lone heron and the threatening clouds below. The shining plane bored ahead of the heron and disappeared with a roar of thunder into the wall of clouds ahead.

On and on the heron beat his way through the slanting, weakening rays of waning sun. Ahead loomed an enormous island sculpted with chains of large peaks—wrinkled sheets of mountains that had never felt the scouring press of glaciers. Iere, Land of the Hummingbird, the Indians had called it. *La Trinité* Columbus had named it, for three hills near the spot where he had anchored in 1498. Trinidad men call it now.

Scarlet ibis, symbol of Trinidad and Tobago.

4
TRINIDAD

A SOMEWHAT REFRESHED GREAT blue heron awoke as the first rays of the sun smiled on him—the same sun that smiled on Africa, on the wide Atlantic, and on the massive waves that crashed upon the shore, unbroken all the way from Africa's shores.

The rugged mountains of Trinidad's Northern Range rose sharply from the sea. Luxuriant tropical rainforest covered the steep slopes, presenting a wall of jungle down to the sea. Great trees roped with vines and lianas carried air plants, bromeliads, and orchids in their tops.

The moisture-laden winds from the east rose over the mountains, cooled, and dropped their showers daily on the green tangle. It was rainy season in the tropics. Leading west along the uninviting northern shore, the great blue rounded a point of land with a scattering of parched, cactus-covered islands. Here in the shadow of the mountains practically no rain fell.

The heron found himself looking down the west coast of the island of Trinidad, across brisk boat traffic and offshore oil rigs busily pumping wealth out of the sea. Blue mountains of Venezuela unfolded across the horizon. Trinidad is a piece of South America set adrift in the Caribbean Sea. A scant eleven thousand years ago, the waters of the mighty Orinoco River erased the lowlands between the mountains and mainland, but biologically her birds, her flowers, her animals still belong to South America.

The capital city, Port of Spain, a typically Caribbean congregation of rusty red roofs, lay before great blue. Not for him the thronging commerce of Frederick Street. The open green space of the Queen's Park Savannah already swarmed with uniformed school children.

It was the mouth of the Caroni swamp beyond which beckoned the weary traveler. On past the processing plants where Nestlé made island cacao beans into chocolate he flew, past the distilleries where island sugarcane was transformed into rum. Open ditches carrying waste products to the swamp led the heron across a smoking dump with a vulture sitting on every fence post, through countryside where East Indians tended their crops. He passed rice paddies diked to keep salt water out, and finally there stretched before him only the dark labyrinth of watery channels through the mangroves. The great Caroni swamp was ready to welcome home the handful of herons which would be wintering there.

The young great blue found new and good fish in the warm estuary waters. A handsome, shiny black crab dotted with white waved its bright red eye stalks at the heron. With an effortless reach of his long neck the bird picked the crab off the mangrove roots.

Strange plants, the mangroves—trees forty feet high or more, standing in the water on stilts. Long aerial roots dangled down to plant in time even more props. Sprouting seeds pointed many inches of stout root, fingers reaching for the water, from the branch tips. The fruits did not fall from the branches, but remained until the seeds had germinated there in the air and the young plants were ready to drop off into the hostile salt waters on their own. Termites built large, dark, rounded homes for their colonies high on the mangrove trunks. Covered tunnels traced pathways up and down the trees, networks of safe passage across the termite world. Pink lichens blotched the tree trunks, rich yellow-gold ones covered the mangrove stilts to the waterline where mangrove oysters tightly clung.

When the heron was well filled, he sought the mangrove shade for a noon siesta. Never had he felt so warm. The humid air weighed heavily upon him. The heron was sleeping fitfully when a torrential downpour suddenly swept the swamp. Hurtling raindrops cratered the soft gray mud left bare by the falling tide. Rivulets of fresh water joined the channels of salt. The swamp was brimming with creatures finely tuned to this combination of sweet and salt.

The shower moved on as quickly as it had come, leaving the air no cooler than before. Softly dripping leaves and swollen channels of rainwater were the only signs of its passing. The sleepy heron was startled by a large, brilliantly crimson bird stepping silently down out of the mangroves to pluck a fiddler crab from the oyster-covered roots. The tough, large gundy claw the bird dexterously removed and cast aside. While that bird was thus occupied with its gundy crab, another equally flaming-scarlet bird dropped down onto the mud flats and set about probing its extraordinary, long, decurved bill into the ooze. Scarlet ibis, national symbol of Trinidad and Tobago. They paid the young heron from Maine no heed and went quietly about their feeding.

Wide awake now, the great blue set out. Narrow channels, quite roofed over with mangroves branched and rejoined, laced in and out the tall stilts. The scarlet ibis could pass through most of the root arches with no difficulty, but the great heron could not. He preferred to fish only the open channels.

The tide at the coast had begun returning water to the swamp. How small the tide fall was compared with the drop in the bay where the heron was born. Large flocks of blue-winged teal deep in the mangrove tangles were dipping, dabbling, quacking softly to each other in the safety of the secret passageways. From New England they came, tracing the same route as great blue. From Canada they came too, from the potholes of the plains of Alberta and Saskatchewan, and from the Great Lakes states, to winter here.

Late afternoon found the young heron fishing on a grassy flat. Overhead an osprey wheeled and called. A number of other herons were fishing near the great blue. Several little blue herons slowly stalked their prey. Immature little blues, white birds, were like great blue making the trip for the first time. Snowy egrets with elegant trailing plumes dashed energetically about, stirring the waters with their black legs, bright yellow feet. The delicately lovely small blue herons with white bellies and rusty necks man knows by the names Trinidad heron, tri-colored heron, or Louisiana heron. They often held their wings out to cut the glare as they caught fish. The birds all went about feeding in their own way; indeed the different kinds of herons in Trinidad coexisted with less friction than the different colors of men were able to manage. A tall, white, great egret posed immobile at the edge of the flock; groups of scarlet ibis stood about completing the colorful picture.

The scene had many admirers. Across the open water chugged flat-bottomed boats filled with people. Paint peeled off some hulls; tour operators' names were still legible in the red and green paint of others. All belched a blue haze of smoke from their decrepit outboard motors. All were skillfully piloted by East Indian men.

One after another the boats gathered at the mangrove fringes as the first egrets and herons began flying in to roost on the green islets. The birds seemed oblivious to the gabbling flocks of people. Guides swapped jokes or dozed against their motors.

"I say, would you care to borrow my insect repellent?"

"It's after five, might the birds not come tonight?"

"Junior honey, come down out of the trees at once. Get back in the boat! RIGHT NOW!"

Binoculars were focused on neighboring boat loads, on circling birds which appeared and disappeared in the clouds above—frigatebirds, the guides said—and on the jets which lifted off from Piarco Airport and disappeared over the misty blue peaks of the Northern Range.

Suddenly in that magic signalless communication that seems to operate in groups of animals of all kinds, the birds began arriving in great numbers, the motors coughed to life, and boats scurried out to the line of poles in the water marking the boundary of the sanctuary.

Little blue herons settled themselves in the top branches. Louisiana herons came winging in low over the water. Great egrets, snowies, and cattle egrets sprinkled themselves liberally through the dark foliage. Two black-crowned night herons flew off complaining loudly to each other on the way to their nocturnal feeding grounds.

A German who had arrived that day on a Russian ship suddenly stood up and shouted, *"Hier kommen die Roten!"*

Winging in to the mangrove hummocks came a loose "Y" of beautiful red birds—the scarlet ibis. Flock after flock came streaming in from their secret haunts throughout the swamps. The dying light of the sun blazed momentarily on the glowing, scarlet birds.

They wheeled, and the new angle presented them as dark shapes against the rosy sunset. The great birds made exotic silhouettes with their curved bills, long necks, strong wings, and trailing legs.

It was a glorious spectacle: the static beauty of the dark mountains, the sheen of the still waters and the twilight sky, animated by hundreds and hundreds of magnificent wild birds—large, incredibly colored, curiously shaped, free, mysterious creations.

The trees filled up with birds.

Night came quickly; hastily the boats withdrew.

Quiet Caroni belonged to the birds.

November came and went. The young great blue heron found Trinidad a satisfactory place to spend the winter and traveled no farther. Others of his kind had found wintering places in the southern United States, in South America, in Central America, and a few birds scattered throughout the West Indies.

Small flocks of brown pelicans skimmed past great blue in single file, low over the water. He saw them fold their wings and dive underwater for fish. Agile white terns darted, dipped, dove around the ponderous brown birds. Anhingas, cormorantlike birds visiting from South America, swam underwater, caught tilapia fish and came up to the surface to swallow them.

Men, too, came to catch the tilapia which they had introduced to these waters. With their hands they caught them. The dikes

around the swamp were marked with circles of charcoal and barbecue spits of sticks, where the East Indians cooked the fish and ate them with macaroni and green figs.

Great blue learned how to hunt for the crabs that riddled the dikes with their burrows. He disappeared into the mangroves whenever a boatload of oyster collectors appeared or when laughing East Indian children came paddling along dipping up crabs with long-handled nets, filling the bottoms of their little boats.

He knew where he could nap undisturbed in the sunshine amid white mangrove orchids, where the tiny green jewel of a pigmy kingfisher darting across the channel would be his only company. The large sleeping heron did not bother Rooti, the yellow-throated spinetail, at its nest tucked away in the black mangroves. Like the others of this exclusively tropical family of birds, the noisy little birds built a large chamber of sticks for a nest and equipped it with an entrance tunnel, like a teapot with a spout.

The tall mangroves standing everywhere on stilts men called "red." "Black" mangroves, growing in the shallowest waters of the swamp, poked slender fingers up out of the mud—specialized air-breathing root tissue. Black mangroves and sedges bordered one side of the dredged bank of the dike; rice, watermelons, and sugarcane stretched away toward the mountains on the other side. Here in the freshly harvested rice fields the heron could hear flocks of dickcissels, the rice birds. These little finches, colored and patterned like miniature meadowlarks, came down from the alfalfa fields of the American prairies to pick the rice seeds from the ground.

Pasturing on the rough grass and wallowing in the silty mud were water buffalo, whose forebears had been imported with the indentured Indians and Chinese brought to harvest sugarcane

The scarlet ibis came to Caroni Sanctuary.

after the black Africans had been freed. On the backs of the water buffalo often rode cattle egrets, which had simply appeared in South America a few decades ago, having made their own way across the ocean from Africa. Wherever livestock trampled up insects from the grasses, the cattle egrets were there to feed. They spent their days following the cattle and the plows in the nearby fields, returning at night to roost in Caroni.

The first men Caroni had ever known were Arawak Indians who silently hunted in the dark mangrove lanes. After Columbus came a small colony of Spaniards, who settled on the banks of the river and grew tobacco to send back to Spain until their small city was sacked and burned in 1595 by adventuring Sir Walter Raleigh. After Raleigh repaired his ships with tarry pitch from the great asphalt lake to the south of Caroni he sailed away, leaving the swamp several centuries of relative quiet. Inevitably, agriculture and commerce came to compete with the swamp. In 1953 Caroni Sanctuary was created for the dwindling populations of scarlet ibis. Nearly five hundred acres were set aside for the exclusive use of the birds that so many tourists come to see, birds that proudly grace the country's coat-of-arms.

The great blue heron, flapping in somber dignity above a group of carmine-hued ibis, headed slowly over the line of stakes in the water at the edge of the sanctuary, out across the swamp to Number Nine drainage canal.

He was the youngest of the Caroni swamp tour operators. He owned his own binoculars. He was proud of them, and proud that he had learned to guide boats through the shallow, twisting, tidal waterways. He could find birds that many of the other boatmen never saw. He was the first to find the nearly perfectly camouflaged potoo, kin to the whippoorwill, that spent the day asleep, upright in a notch in a mangrove tree. He knew where Rooti the spinetail hid its teakettle nest. He knew the ways of all the birds and he loved them. Like all the other tour operators, he knew that the welfare of the herons, the egrets, and the ibis—the well-being of the great swamp itself—was directly linked with his own.

He had been uneasy when he heard the shots as he went out to take cartons of sweet drinks to the boatloads of tourists waiting for the ibis to come in. He himself had had no customers and was planning to do some exploring after his errand. He could see several groups of ibis wheel up in flight and circle away.

"Joe-Joe, you got he, sure!" the young guide heard as two more shots rang out just across the dike from where he was. But by the time his own boat rounded the bend, the would-be hunters were disappearing in hasty retreat at the sound of his motor. It was open season. They were probably hunting blue-winged teal—why did they flee?

A ripple in the water in the mangroves caught his eye. It was a large bird struggling weakly. A great blue heron, the wary "crane" the hunters could not resist, was lying in the water, staining it with blood. Its wing appeared damaged and the waterlogged bird was nearly drowned.

Gently the young guide lifted the bird into his boat. It was not the first time he had had to dry off one of the heron family and replace it in the safety of the mangroves. This bird would need more attention than that, however. Other men had succeeded in reviving injured birds. He would take it home and try. Besides, his younger brother Ram would love it. Ram could hardly wait till he was old enough to become a guide.

The guide carefully rearranged the injured wing and sponged blood off the bird. Such a wonderful long neck, soft gray and brown, handsomely spotted with black and pale tones of russet. Its gray wing covert feathers bore white spots and a delicate edging of cinnamon. Its thighs were the same rich, pinkish-cinnamon color. Sadly he noted that this was yet a young bird. It lacked the crest and body plumes of mature birds. Some great blues were said to live twenty years, but the young man was not confident that this bird would live through one.

It was nearly dark when he arrived back at the dock at the edge of the swamp. He could barely see the bats that fluttered, feeding, above the canal. The lights of the propane gas depot shone on his cousin's shiny new taxi waiting for him. His cousin did not care to drive his new taxi in the busiest part of the rush hour in Port of Spain. He would be glad to see the guide, but the bloody bird would not be welcome to ride in the automobile.

After much protest, the cousin produced some of his polishing cloths and a few sacks from the car's trunk. He frowned as he retrieved the plastic lovebirds that fell to the spotless carpet when the guide climbed in the back seat with his burden. The cousin had been happy to drive many good-paying fares up and down the mountains from Caroni to the Arima Valley where the Asa Wright Nature Center was. He liked the people who came to see the birds of Trinidad, so he chided his young cousin but he drove him home, not even stopping at the cricket game as he had intended.

Ram was too excited to speak when his big brother gave him the wounded heron. Fighting back the tears as they dressed the great bird's wing, Ram begged to be allowed to spend the night with the wounded bird. At dawn's first light he sent the poor bird into a panic with his shout of glee when he discovered that the bird was on its feet. Ram beat a quick retreat as the big bird struck at his head.

Diligently, he netted fish for the heron. Pails and pails of them he gathered. He tried feeding great blue mice and insects and even scraps of rotis, hard round bread he had saved from breakfast. His brother promised to write a letter to the people who knew about the numbers on the silver band on the heron's leg. Ram twisted off the yellow spiral band and wore it as a ring on his finger.

The new home for the great blue heron was an empty animal shed. Rains thundered daily on its corrugated tin roof. Feed sacks stretched along the chicken-wire sides completed the job of keeping the heron dry and relatively unbothered by the scrawny, long-legged hound dogs that abound in Trinidad. By spending many hours quietly with the wounded young bird, Ram in time gained the heron's tolerance. His brother helped him fix a soft leather jess on the heron's ankle so that a leash could be fastened on and the bird could enjoy the relative freedom of outings in the gardens and fields.

Ram's family, like so many other East Indians in the villages outside of Port of Spain, rented acre blocks in the Arrangues estate for gardens. When Ram rose early to get the day's water from the standpipe at the corner, the heron knew just what events would follow. From his shelter the heron could see the boy impatiently twisting poinsettia leaves as he waited for the trickle from the spigot.

"Qu'est ce qu'il dit?" shouted a raucous yellow, black, and brown kiskadee from the top of a pink poui tree. The cocky bird darted down to pick a lizard from the trunk of a banana plant. The first hummingbirds were feeding in the blue vervain in the yard. An aggressive little ruby topaz buzzed by; the copper rump of a common emerald gleamed in the sun as the tiny bird, chirping softly to itself, probed one blossom after another. The boy loved to watch the hummers, but the inviting aroma of cocoa tea and roasting eggplant and tomatoes lured him back to breakfast just as his mother came to the door looking impatiently for the boy and the water.

"Coming, moomah," Ram called.

Before the sun was hot the family would be working in their garden carefully tying tomatoes up on trellises of bamboo, weeding, trimming with cutlasses, as they called their machetes. Sometimes Ram would take the heron down to the rows of the adjacent pineapple plantation. From the center of each rosette of daggerlike leaves sprouted a young pineapple fruit, itself crowned by yet another spiny whorl of leaves. The heron would often find himself tied in the shade of a cashew tree. From the spreading green branches hung bright red fruits, specialized flower stalk tissue from the end of which protruded the funny twisted nuts. Cashews, native to Trinidad, looked to Ram like the mangrove roosts of scarlet ibis, complete with the flashy red birds.

Clouds covered and uncovered the lofty mountains of the Northern Range, traffic streamed along the road into Port of Spain.

Two-wheeled carts of produce creaked along behind little donkeys oblivious to the honking taxis. Roadside roti stands opened up along the highways, and other vendors did a brisk business selling corn roasted on charcoal braziers by the side of the pavement. Ancient crones with bright, knotted bandanas bobbing gaily above their withered dark faces squatted beside neat piles and pyramids of melons, bananas, and coconuts.

At the end of the day the human tide would turn. Workers would return from their fields. From Port of Spain the traffic would swarm out to the little villages. Finally even the vendors would pack up and go home, until the morrow, when it would all begin again.

A day came when the routine was not like the others. The heron sensed that Ram was excited when the boy came to feed him. Ram seemed eager for great blue to eat. The big bird did his best to oblige but finally had to turn away from one flapping fish presented to him. The heron's wing was mending nicely, his strength returning. The bird spent more and more hours pacing in his pen or straining at his leash and exercising his big wings when they went out to the gardens. Perhaps he would soon get his freedom.

That was not what Ram had in mind this day, however. The boy did not return until late in the afternoon and then he came by truck. When the rattling plank-sided truck ground to a dusty halt in the yard, Ram hopped out of the back. The whole family appeared and began putting things in the truck. Ram fastened the leash onto the heron and let him step out of the pen. The heron blinked a moment in the sunlight. He let out a loud squawk when Ram's brother grabbed his bill with one hand, pulled a sack over the bird, and unceremoniously lifted him into the back of the truck.

There, among the watermelons and bundles and cloth sacks, was Ram. The boy spoke softly, comfortingly, and put his arm around the cloth-covered, trembling bird. If only the great blue heron could have understood as Ram explained to him that the family was going up into the mountains for the weekend to help Ram's uncle harvest coffee. At first Ram's family had objected to taking the ungainly bird with them. Ram's big brother had agreed with Ram that it would be a few more weeks until the heron was healed enough to return to the swamp. Most assuredly, if the heron were left at home alone he would be in someone's cooking pot before the family returned.

As they clattered along the busy highway, a girl Ram knew waved her cutlass in greeting as they passed her garden. A man eating a roti called a greeting and a joke to Ram's father when the traffic paused in front of one of the high houses that had a snackette built under it at ground level. From under another house a goat bleated at them and the hound dogs on the porch above set up a barking. The heron shuddered.

Soon the lights of Arima were twinkling around them. A cricket game was still in session in the savanna. The soft, mellow sounds of steel drums came tinkling on the warm evening air from the pan yard where the men were practicing their new songs for Carnival. The streets of Arima were filled with black people of all ages. Girls in bright dresses paraded past gangs of young men in knitted caps of every imaginable color combination. Older men in baggy trousers stood in small groups under the street lamps smoking and talking and arguing together. Women appeared and disappeared into stores and called across the street to one another. Everyone, it seemed, was out enjoying the cool hours of the fleeting day.

As the road wound up the valley from the town, a silky darkness closed in. Now and then headlights of the truck picked up the solemn gaze of lone donkeys tethered to graze along the roadside until they were needed once again in the morning for pulling the carts of fruits and vegetables down from the hills to market. Back and forth the truck zigged and zagged and bounced as the narrow, potholed road climbed higher into the mountains. At last the glow of lights on the miniature temple in the little East Indian settlement above Arima signaled to Ram that they were nearly there. A few more bends and the terrifying ride was over for great blue.

Cousins, aunts, and uncles swarmed out of the little tapia house, its walls made of split bamboo, plastered with mud, and painted a friendly pink. They crowded around the heron, exclaiming over his size and beauty. Great blue was panting with fright and fatigue by the time sleeping quarters were found for him. The roof of the drying shed was rolled closed, cacao beans were pushed into a corner, and the heron was shut inside.

Long after the occupants of the house had gone to sleep, frogs filled the air with their choruses and the stars of the Southern Cross appeared above the horizon, but still the heron did not sleep. Like the cry of a haunting night spirit came the soft hooting of the jumbie bird, the pygmy owl—ten, twenty, thirty times the same note. Old

The soft cry of the pygmy owl floated through the night air.

Granny who sold coconuts down in the valley by the gardens had told Ram about the jumbie who has no head, no feet. At night when you are out you hear it coming behind you. Your head gets bigger and bigger and you can hardly run. But you throw a handful of sand across your trail and it will stop and count each grain. When she thought perhaps the little East Indian boy did not believe the old black, she shook a gnarled finger in his face and said, "You don't think the old head knows, boy, but you see something white on the path like a sheet, it is the jumbie. You walk across it and they will sure sure find you on the rocks in the morning." There were men in these hills who would kill an owl if they could. To them the soft monotone cry in the night was a fearful sound; to the heron, perhaps it seemed consoling. He crooked his neck in a tight "S" resting his head on his feathers, and slept.

Long before the sun itself peered over the mountains, the sky brightened with the coming of day. It might rain once today, or not at all. Dry season had begun.

A yelping call like a puppy off in the distance brought Ram scurrying out of the house. The toucans were calling in the top of the myristica trees on the hill beyond the house. Dexterously they picked the tiny fruits with their large, black-and-pale-blue bills.

Ram slipped quietly into the drying shed and greeted his great blue heron. During the sunny hours of the day the shed always stood open to dry the beans of cacao or coffee. But at night, or whenever a shower threatened to wet the drying harvest, the roof could be quickly slid back. He rolled the tin roof back along its track and he and the heron hopped down to the ground. Ram brought the heron breakfast from the truck—some dead fish.

Between the house and the forest itself was an orchard of sorts. Ram helped himself to a grapefruit from one of the trees. He sat down under a cacao tree, peeled and ate the sweet juicy grapefruit. He offered a section to the heron but the bird refused it.

The cacao trees resembled no trees great blue had seen before. Their trunks were spotted with lichens, their branches furred with epiphytes. Starry white blossoms on short stems grew directly out of the bark of the trunk, where pollinating insects would be sure to see them. A few nearly ripe yellow or mahogany-red pods hung along the trunk. Most of the pods had been recently hacked off with machetes or with poles tipped with a knife blade tied on by Ram's uncle and his family. They had opened the pods, removed the neat rows of seeds from the slimy white pith, fermented the beans, and dried them in the cacao shed. Bags and bags of cacao beans were awaiting the trip to the Nestlé plant down in the valley.

Leaving the heron tethered to a cacao tree, Ram hurried back to the house in answer to his aunt's call. Sunlight streamed on the golden blossoms of the immortelle trees which protected the cacao trees with their shade. From the treetops came trumpetings, rattles, and wheezes, the sound of a steel band—all of it from large, black birds with long, handsome, yellow tails—oropendolas. They fed on the blossoms and flew back and forth over the little orchard to the tree where their nests hung. No less bizarre than their songs were their nests—a dozen or so long bags hanging from immortelle branches. Like the orioles of North America, these South American relations build pendulous nests—only these were five feet long, swaying gently above the fretful heron.

When Ram returned with his cousins, tall black rubber boots flapped about their slender legs to protect them from the deadly bushmaster. They had no desire to meet mapepire, the large reddish brown-and-gray banded snake of not very pleasant temper, but they brandished their cutlasses boldly, told each other lies, and headed gaily up the road with picking sacks tied around their waists, a couple of wicker baskets, and a great blue heron struggling on a leash.

Stripping the ripe, red coffee beans into the pouch at his waist was pleasant work for Ram. In many ways he envied his mountain cousins. He eyed the little green nutmegs in the branches of the trees overhead and sighed. Come Easter, his cousins would walk the road every morning and pick up the ripe nutmegs that had fallen to the ground. So much easier a harvest than chopping prickly pineapples or cutting sugarcane! The plump, pale yellow-green husks of the nutmegs would split open and pop off easily, revealing the bright crimson network of mace that surrounded the shiny brown nutmeg within.

At a bend in the road they surprised a pair of jacamars dust-bathing in the gravel. King hummers Ram's cousins called them, as the glowing, green birds swooped daringly close to the boys. They did look like hummingbirds with their long thin beaks and iridescent colors—except these kings were ten inches long.

Ram stopped under an overhanging tree limb to peer up into the shade for a glimpse of an even more colorful bird that softly called its name: a motmot. The double hooting ceased abruptly. A red eye glared down at the boys. Like the jacamars, its breast was chestnut and its back an emerald green, but its crown and its tail were a gorgeous royal blue. Usually a motmot can outstare any passerby, but the tall heron standing underneath disturbed the bird. It began to twitch its long blue tail back and forth like a pendulum. The round racquetlike tips, suspended as if by fine wires where the barbs had worn off the shafts, quivered on the long pair of tail feathers.

Ram hurried to catch up with his cousins who had left the little winding road and turned up an even narrower trace, or path. He stopped to look at the eggs in a nest he found plastered just at eye level on the red clay of the bank. Three green-blue eggs he counted in the mossy cup belonging to the cocoa thrush. He stopped again to answer the collared trogon calling "cyow-cyow-cyow" sweet-sadly in the treetops. The gorgeous, green-and-scarlet bird sat still as an air plant, its long, black-and-white barred tail hanging straight down, blending with leaf shadows. The bird turned only its head and sent its call like a ventriloquist, now here, now over there; and the boy never saw it at all.

"Hoot-hoot-hoot-hoot" like a pygmy owl called Ram and the trogon answered. Small blue honeycreepers hopping about the bushes on bright red legs came with their green mates to see what was going on. While he picked the coffee that grew only in light of the path edge, the boy whistled to cock-of-the-woods, the little black-faced antthrush, which replied from the forest floor where it was busily snapping up insects fleeing from a foraging band of army ants. Although his basket filled slowly, his cousins liked their relative who talked to the birds.

The heron did not feel at ease in the jungle of the rainforest. The peculiar ringing "tack" call of the bearded bellbirds clanged all about them. Hours and hours the male birds spent calling to each other. Tremendously tall trees filtered out the sunlight with their leafy crowns like so many layers of umbrellas. The heron could hear bright-colored birds calling and feeding on the fruits in the sunlight far above but he could not see them.

No two trees above the heron from the north were alike; no two birds seemed the same kind. Whereas his Maine islands possessed fewer than two hundred different kinds of birds in all, Trinidad alone had four hundred; neighboring Venezuela two or three times that number.

The lofty piers of trees were draped and coiled and hung with woody vines, lianas of every description: endless straight ropes, thorny cables, twisting ribbons. Ferns grew everywhere: on the ground, in the tree crowns, vining out on branches, assuming tree forms where light permitted.

Strangler figs grew downward from the sunlit tops of trees, enveloping and smothering their hosts when their roots finally reached the ground. The silvery boles of the forest trees were blotched with lichens in all shades of gray and green, pink ones where the algae partners of the fungus were replaced by bacteria. Great buttress roots spread out from the bases of many of the strange trees on the shadowy forest floor. And it was a most efficient ecosystem. The trees spread their roots shallowly beneath the surface of the soil. In the heat and humidity, dead leaves and dead animals were returned to the cycle of the living almost overnight by the bacterial and fungal decomposers. Before the rains could leach away the precious nutrients, they were absorbed by the rootlets and restored to the lush web of growth.

Much more to the heron's liking was the mountain stream where the boys decided to lunch and swim. Ram studied the unhappy heron. He had saved the heron's life by mending its wing, had he not? He loved the great bird as a pet. Did he love it enough to let it go out of his life? On the stream bank the heron flapped its wings unevenly, teetering awkwardly before it caught its balance. Ram could put off deciding about the heron for a little bit longer. He frowned and tossed a mango pit into the stream.

When the boys returned to their work, the heron caught a few crayfish and a red mountain crab that was eating orange berries in the path. He retired for a nap to the shadows of bananalike heliconias on the bank, surrounded by white-flowered begonias, ferns as tall as he, and huge elephant-eared caladiums. A loop of green vine above the heron's head began to uncoil. It was a six-foot-long tree boa. The heron seemed to consider trying to catch the snake and eat it. Perhaps wisely, instead, he moved back out to the stream bank.

Great blue's keen ears caught the high-pitched cry of a hawk soaring above the ravine. He froze, sleeked his feathers, crouched slightly, and eyed the sky. Above him presently appeared a black hawk, entirely black except for a single white tailband. Not one hawk but two appeared soaring one above the other in the opening above the trees. Suddenly the lower bird rolled over in midair, touched talons briefly with its courting mate, and the pair soared on down the valley. Theirs were the piles of crab shells the heron had found at the stream side, earning them the nickname crab hawk. Before long they would have to spend all their hours hunting crabs to feed their young. But not today. Today must come first.

While the heron watched, a wind began to pick up. It ruffled silver foliage on the peak across the ravine. The silvery leaves of the cecropia, or trumpet tree, dancing in the wind indicated second growth, that the hilltop had in the past been burned and cleared for a garden patch. Here man had grown corn perhaps, high enough up the mountain that even in the dry season the crop would prosper. Tropical gardens came and went, soon to be reclaimed by the forest. Anything more threatened to deplete the scant resources of the soil permanently, leaving it barren and open to erosion.

Great chains of rain beat down. Gloomy darkness fell like a curtain over the forest; mists made of the valley a swirling cauldron. The rains poured down, and passed on. Every waxy evergreen leaf in the forest shed the water, drop after drop, from its spined tip. Rain filled leafy cups in the whorled bases of pineapple1ike brome1iads in the treetops. Frogs which had never set foot on the earth in their lives came there to deposit their eggs.

A rainbow spanned the valley, ending in a gleam in the branches of a blossoming yellow poui tree. Blue-gray tanagers, the color of the distant mountain in the mist, appeared, feeding in the golden blossom bells, and silver-beaked tanagers, wine-red shading into coal black. Brightly bloomed the dripping forest.

Ram and his cousins reappeared with dry clothes and full baskets. The merry party carefully made its way down the slippery red clay paths. The boys threatened to trip each other, to push each other. They dared and they teased, but woe to him who had the misfortune to slip and spill the precious coffee anywhere except on the floor of the drying shed.

Where the trace rejoined the road, the boys stopped to pick and eat the fruit and nuts of the feathery cocorite palms. A gurgle of song, a torrent of squeaky chatter, drew Ram to the edge of the clearing. He heard the kit-kit calls of cocoa thrushes, the whistling of a black-faced antthrush, a little wren, and boat-billed kiskadees—all coming from one bamboo cage hanging in a tree.

How could this be?

The cage was a trap. As a decoy in the innermost compartment sat a little, green, female euphonia, or semp. And pouring his heart out in the trap was the clever mimic, one beautiful male euphonia. He was a shiny purple-black with a golden-yellow cap and breast, and he was destined to spend the rest of his days singing for a scrap of rotten banana in a cage under the eaves of someone's little tapia house.

To Ram that seemed too unjust to bear. He stood admiring the handsome little wildlings and considered setting them free. He knew his cousins would not approve; they, after all, occasionally turned their slingshots on mountain doves and the beautiful thrushes. And perhaps it was stealing. Someone had put the trap here. They had a perfect right to do so as long as they observed the season of the wildlife ordinance. But in the boy's heart he suddenly felt it was more surely stealing to take a wild thing from the place where it lives free.

He reached for the door fastening of the cage.

A hand gripped viciously on his shoulder and spun him around. A gaunt man in tattered clothes snarled at him. Four long-legged hounds on rawhide leashes, no less gaunt than their master, snarled at him. The man tugged angrily at the battered felt hat barely covering his frizzled gray hair. He unbuckled the machete from his belt and, waving it menacingly at the boy, began to shout in Ram's face. He shook his fist and waved his arms. The veins in his neck stood out in blue-black cords.

What did the little coolie boy have to say, he wanted to know. Eh, boy? Going to steal the semps in broad daylight, right here on the road. All those others had seen it. He wasn't going to get away with it.

The man had seen the coffee baskets and Ram's cousins but until his dogs showed him, he had not seen the tall heron tethered by the cocorite palms. He studied the great bird in amazement. He dug his bony fingers into Ram's shoulder as he announced in fiendish glee that the boy would forfeit that bird.

Ram let out a sobbing protest; his cousins looked at each other in fear and confusion. The man turned from Ram to the heron. The great blue at bay stamped nervously and swung his massive bill ready to strike the dogs that were advancing with stiff legs and bristling tails. The cutlass hissed through the air. A shout rang out.

It was Ram's brother. He had come walking down the road, a basket of coffee beans balanced on his head, his shiny binoculars bumping gently on his chest with every step. He heard just enough to know that his little brother needed him.

At the sight of Ram's brother the angry man put his cutlass back in its sheath and pulled his dogs back a safe distance from the heron. The boys were astonished to hear his furious bellowings turn to wheedling and whining. The two men talked, gestured, and nodded.

Ram's heart beat less wildly. He drew a deep breath when he heard his brother scold the man for frightening the boys. Surely that would start the ranting once more. Instead, he saw his brother shake his head and press a coin into the old man's palm. He picked up his coffee and signaled to the boys to do the same.

The old man slung an empty cage on his back and he and his dogs limped off up the hill. Ram, his brother, his cousins, and a ruffled great blue heron headed down the hill.

Carnival! All Trinidad throbbed with the excitement of it. It was a busy time for Ram's family. At their stand in the Queen's Park Savannah in Port of Spain, they sold hundreds of curry-filled rotis, bags and bags of polouri and kachouri, balls and patties of chickpeas expertly fried in coconut oil by Ram's mother. Ram passed out sweet drinks, coconut candies, and green mango pickles to endless throngs of carnival spectators, to the calypsonians and steel bandsmen, to glittering men and women in swirling, glowing, gorgeous costumes. The music and parading seemed endless; on Saturday and Sunday they chose the Calypso King and the Carnival King and Queen. Monday, *Jour Ouvert*, they began at dawn, and Tuesday still no one seemed to tire. Ram was thrilled by the gay music, the sea of people that flowed in and out of the savannah, past the gingerbread Victorian mansions where people watched the grand march from lacy balconies.

Then came Ash Wednesday and the beginning of Lent; Carnival was over for another year. Ram and his family were very tired when they finally dismantled their stand, took down the awning

*The old man and his dogs
limped off up the hill.*

with YE OLDE TAJ MAHAL printed on it, packed everything into the truck, and went back to their home in the country.

Ram's sister had promised to take care of the heron while he was away. It was not her fault, she said, that the bird had disappeared. She was sure she had fastened the door of the shed each time, and besides, Ram had agreed to take the bird back to the swamp at the end of this week anyway.

Ram paced back and forth in front of the deserted shed. He slammed the wire door. He could not bear to look in the shadows where no heron waited. He turned to the sky and tried to imagine how it was. He was the heron pacing a never ending circuit. One time someone opened the door. Or the wind blew it. Or a wire broke. One time, and the heron was gone.

Had a pack of dogs or a hungry neighbor waited outside the door? Ram preferred to picture the heron free. Its beautiful wings whole at long last, the heron had lifted off. Over the housetops he had soared. Higher and higher, free, into the air. Away. But it

A jaçana family foraging.

76

grieved the boy that he never really knew what became of his great blue heron.

Gray ashes dropped softly down out of the evening sky, ashes from the black columns billowing out of the cane fields. Ripe cane stalks waved feathery white plumes atop fifteen-feet-high stems, like giant corn tassels on grass flowers, a vast sea of silver at the foot of the green mountain. Men sent fires racing through the sugarcane the night before they cut it—to get rid of the snakes they said, and the sharp spines on the leaf blades. Ashes rained down on the ibis in their mangrove roosts in Caroni swamp, on the mud-covered water buffalo wallowing in their pastures on the Caroni plain, on fluffy jaçana chicks learning to forage in dark square beds of watercress, on a great blue heron standing motionless in a tall grove of bamboo.

Day after day great blue found himself becoming more restless and ill at ease. His stiff wing bothered him less. His gaunt body began to fill out with the excellent fishing of the great complex of swamps and wet agricultural lands. As the days gained minutes from the nights, equaled and then surpassed them, the young heron began to accumulate fat deposits under his skin. His feathers, once again clean and well-groomed, began to regain their silky sheen. His legs took on a richer olive hue. The glow of health had returned to his eye, but it did not bring him peace.

True, he fished as patiently as ever. During the many hours he spent staring motionless at the water, great blue came to know well the little jaçana family. It was the male jaçana that had incubated the three brown eggs in the floating nest. The father bird led the chicks off across the water when they were only a few days old. Their feet looked as if they were borrowed from bigger birds, their toe span equal to the length of their whole body. On these marvelous, slender, straight toes the whole family of jaçanas stepped effortlessly over the lily pads. Gallinules also walked over the water weeds in the Trinidad swamps, but the jaçanas had the further distinction of reptilelike spurs on their wings like ancient

Archeopteryx, the earliest bird fossil man knows. The young jaçanas fluttered their golden-lined wings and flew like their parents. Full of youthful vitality, they were not goaded by the restlessness that had overtaken the young great blue heron.

The cattle egrets that lived in the swamp and hunted the meadows had a different look about them these days. Hunting along a drainage ditch one day, great blue met a male whose feathers were delicately tinged with tawny buff. The bird began to snap his bill and erect his glowing plumes. This aggressive-looking full forward display was not directed at the great blue heron, but at a female cattle egret. The male picked up a twig and shook it. He raised his crest feathers and stretched out his long neck, whereupon the other bird stepped up behind him and struck him a blow with her bill. She clung to his back and hit his head again and again with her own. Such is love among the cattle egrets, but the young great blue watched impassively. It would be another year before sexual longings stirred him.

He was more moved by the restless chattering of the barn swallows in the evenings. They spent the last hours of the day picking insects out of the air above the refuse heaps of bagasse, the sugarcane stalks that had been squeezed of their sweet juice. As the sun went down, the barn swallows gathered on utility wires; the flocks twittered on into the gathering dusk in unwonted animation.

The great blue heron uneasily eyed the skeins of small birds tracing long columns across the fading sun. By the hundreds and thousands, the dickcissels came from the rice fields to roost in the sugarcane. They bent the cane leaves with their numbers and filled the air with their strange roosting calls. From a hundred thousand throats came the tiny sounds, united, swelling, enveloping the cane fields in an anxious colossal hissing.

As darkness, sugarcane ashes, and quiet fell upon the Caroni plain, the great blue heron unwillingly settled himself among the bamboos. Several times the great invisible city of dickcissels in the cane before him broke out into ripples of communication. Stars appeared over the Northern Range and then their twinkling disappeared from the cloudless sky as wave after wave of dark bird forms lifted off silently from the cane. The dickcissels were leaving. Flock after flock of the hundreds and thousands of Trinidad's rice birds masked the night sky with their exodus. They were going back to the North American prairies.

They were gone.

One day the barn swallows, too, were gone. The telephone wires would hang bare in the sky along the cane fields for a few weeks until the blue-and-white swallows came up from Argentina to escape the blasts of winter at the other end of the continent.

For some time now the lengthening periods of daylight had signaled that it was time for herons to begin their migration. Half his life the young bird had spent in Trinidad, and now it was time to head back to the north and take up once more his other existence. The hormones in his blood passed the signals along to the rest of his body, but because of his period of captivity, the young heron's body was, for a time, not ready to go. Fair winds came and went, until at last his healed body answered the summons of a passing ridge of high pressure, and great blue headed north.

The man leaning against the coconut palm by the beach whacked the coconuts one after another in the palm of his hand with his cutlass, tossed the white meats into the drying shed, the husks and shells to the waiting black vultures. A large blue-spotted lizard dashed into the dark beneath the copra shed.

In the town the doors and windows stood open to the breezes. The church in the tiny village of Blanchisseuse on the north coast of Trinidad was still decorated with the palms and purple cloth from Palm Sunday. An old woman was slowly sweeping in the cool shadows inside the church.

A woman in a clean, faded-yellow dress, neat scarf knotted about her head, wordlessly followed down the mountain her husband, who walked beside their short-legged gray donkey piled high with bundles. Their bare feet softly slapped the dust of the well-worn trace.

The ringing melody of "Ave Maria" rose up on the morning sunshine to greet the walkers. Passionately, powerfully, a woman was singing to herself in one of the pastel huts. The beautiful sound filtered out through the gingerbread wooden lace of the white ventilator panels, engulfed the chattering euphonia in the cage on the flower-draped piazza, rose above the jetlike whine of invisible cicadas in the treetops and soared over the laughter and gossip of the women doing their laundry in the river.

From her nest attached to the underside of a palm frond that hung out over the water, a rufous-breasted hermit hummingbird watched the shadow of a great blue heron sweep down across the pebbled riverbed.

As the heron passed, a man paused in the pinwheel whirling of his arm that was to have carried his fishing line out into the current. Several of the naked children bathing downstream from their mothers turned to watch the great bird wing out over the sandbar that partially blocked the mouth of the Marianne River from the sea.

Only the tiny green pygmy kingfisher sunning in the top of the bamboos saw the big heron become a tiny speck resolutely aimed in the direction of Tobago, Grenada, the Grenadines. Stroking steadily in low leisurely beats, great blue disappeared into the distance.

Great blue at St. Vincent.

5
ST. VINCENT

LIKE THE TAIL OF a kite the tiny islands of the Grenadines strung south from St. Vincent. Trailing toward the equator for forty miles to Union and Petit St. Vincent, Canouan, Mustique, Bequia, and dozens of small islands, the chain marked where the ancient ocean floor was split by volcano after volcano, the Antilles in miniature. The trade winds sailed over the lowest islands without giving up their moisture, leaving the islands dry and bare. Where sufficient moisture fell for growing sugarcane, the ruins of mills and Great Houses stood among the resorts and estates. Airstrips crossed some of the islands from one side to the other. Bright yachts plied the shining waters.

From almost every isle and islet, gay dancing kites greeted the heron. It was Good Friday—Kite Day throughout the Caribbean, even up to Bermuda. Kites dangled from telephone wires and tugged upward from every hill. The kites of St. Vincent were small, regular hexagons beckoning like parti-colored flowers above the lush greenery. The little boys on the cricket fields flew their kites with one hand and chewed on fragrant hot cross buns.

Freighters were busy loading bananas at the long wharfs of Kingstown. The forested peaks of Grand Bonhomme and Petit Bonhomme were hidden by clouds. The cactus-fringed leeward coast seemed uninviting to the great blue heron so he doubled back to the southernmost tip of the island and dropped down to a quiet cove.

Heavy breakers smashed on living banks of coral reefs, glowing violet under the turquoise waters. Tamed, the gentle rollers poured themselves out in creamy succession on the shore of golden coral sand. A fringe of coconut palms cast their barred shadows on the unoccupied beach.

The heron caught one of St. Vincent's variety of speckled crab. He stood a long time staring into water that brought him no fish. A flicker of foam and flashing bodies just beyond the reefs showed that a school of flying fish was passing by. Out of the blue appeared a frigatebird, a young bird, dark, with a white head and bib. Deftly it snatched one of the fish from the surface with its hooked bill and tossed its head back to swallow its catch. The scissor-tailed form of a coal-black, adult male hurtled down out of the sky, bent on piracy. The young bird maneuvered gallantly. Its attacker struck with powerful bill; its giant wings pummeled the fish-carrying bird. The younger bird struck back, but in so doing dropped the quarry. Before either of the large sea birds could claim the prize, the great blue heron settled the squabble with a lunge and a gulp.

From around the point silently appeared a small lateen-rigged sailboat, its sail gleaming a rich buff in the late afternoon sun. The arrival of the craft was a signal. The beach came suddenly to life with laughing children. Great blue flapped off to the shelter of sea grapes on the rocky wall of the cove, his dark form invisible against the black volcanic rocks.

As he watched, the boat sailed up onto the beach. The half dozen men hopped out. They ferried black, watermelon like ballast rocks ashore, then carried the hull across the wet sand to the back of the beach. Another sail appeared, and another. An old sow came trotting out of the shade followed by two pink and scrawny piglets. Grunting and squeaking, they rooted around through the piles of fish guts tossed on the beach. Women carrying bags and baskets appeared to buy the red snapper, the glistening king, and jack, and thick steaks of shark meat.

Almost as quickly as it had begun, the drama on the beach came to an end. Children gave up trying to knock down the long-stemmed green mangoes from the tree. Men and women drifted back up the hill leaving the beach to the pigs. A lady trudged up the road with the bole of a palm tree resting on her bandana-wrapped skull. Friends called to her from the open sides of the passing bus that came rumbling up the narrow road and disappeared into the hills for the night.

Small boys bringing home the herd for the night struggled to pull nanny goats to the sides of the road out of the traffic, while even tinier kids struggled to nurse in spite of the commotion.

Youngsters carried square five-gallon water cans or ragged bundles of firewood on their heads up the hills to home.

In the yard above the heron's shelter a woman was cooking a pot of rice over coals in an oil drum while her daughter took in the dry laundry spread on the bushes of a hibiscus hedge.

A sleek yawl came gliding by in a whisper. It joined a handful of similar vessels moored at the end of the cove that served as yacht basin.

The sun dropped quickly into the sea on the far side of the island, scarcely coloring the evening sky before the darkness fell. Moonlight silhouetted the pale candelabra of blooms and lance leaves of agave. Sea grapes waved dark circles across the sand. The dark fin of a shark cut the silver moon path on the water at reef's edge. The reef itself was alive with the swaying of the myriad tiny coral polyps feeding in the gentle surge. Dark schools of tiny fish nosed here and there. While some fish hung suspended and immobile in the crevices of the reef, others were fighting, courting, living, and dying in the warm, dark waters. Tiny pinpoints of light marked some mysterious disturbance among the plankton which responded with flashes of phosphorescence.

The wind rose and fell, palms rustled and were silent. All night through, always, the sea whispered to the shore.

As the sky lightened with the dawn, the great blue heron awoke and stretched. He unfolded one great wing, spread it full and down. He extended that long leg, stretched to the top of his toes, and shifted his weight to stretch the other side. The heron bobbed his head and stood a few moments regarding the sunlight gleaming on the white freighter bound for Kingstown. Across the horizon, Bequia still loomed in purple darkness. Piles of lavender-and-gold clouds were already making their way in from the sea to crown Bequia, Island of the Clouds. Before long the clouds would come skimming westward to rise and rain on St. Vincent.

Fishing boats began to appear and disappear in the troughs between the waves. A group of men in ranks rowed a heavy boat across the harbor. Sunlight caressed the gleaming hulls of sleek yachts slumbering at anchor. Morning breezes playing in the stays sounded softly against the metal masts.

At the far end of the beach, a handful of black children bathed and played at the water's edge, their mommas gossiping barefoot in the sand before going off to work. The sun bathed the hill behind them in yellow-olive greens, lit the pastel houses and fence posts topped with dainty orchids up where the rooster crowed, ignited flashes of magenta bougainvillea vines defying the black-greens of the tropics.

The tide was low. Just a few feet offshore, the waves lapped a coral platform. Some twenty feet farther out ramparts of elkhorn and fire corals rose from the sea. The waves foamed through the "antlers" that all pointed toward the shore. The surf spent its force in thickets of staghorn and finger corals. This garden of the sea sheltered many tasty fishes but they were safe from great blue herons.

The shore reef, however, looked promising. The heron spread his great fanning wings, touched down tentatively on the mosslike mat of brown-and-green algae. Satisfied, he folded his feathery cloak around him and began to hunt.

The old coral flat was riddled with tunnels. Every cranny was occupied by a small sea urchin, either red or black, or huge, brown West Indian chitons. Where bits of broken chiton armor tumbled in the wave wash, their inner surfaces glimmered aquamarine. Spidery-armed brittle starfish clinging to the ceilings of the miniature caves also wore this hauntingly beautiful brown-and-blue color combination. Baby tooth snails grazed on the meadows of unicellular algae which coated the reef top. A striped yellow-and-brown moray eel poked its sinister, pointed snout out of its lair. Quickly it withdrew to the shelter of its coral cave before the heron could strike.

The motion of a panicked speckled crab scuttling away betrayed it. Great blue grasped it, dashed it on the reef, and swallowed it whole. Bits of shell and flesh that dropped off the shelf immediately attracted small fish. The heron lowered his head, poised like a spear, and darted out to pick up several small, black fish. The great blue heron stepped soundlessly along the reef. He picked several of the ubiquitous yellow-and-black striped sergeant majors from a fleeing school. He stabbed at a butterfly fish. The fish darted off backward. The heron had been fooled by the false eyespot on its tail.

Water began to trickle across the top of the reef; the tide had turned. Rust-colored anemones expanded once again to dangle flowerlike tentacles in the food-bringing waves. Huge barnacles erupted in feathery flickering, their conical shells as big as thimbles, thickly covered with the precipitated calcium carbonates of encrusting algae. Incoming seas washed the glistening, puckered forms of living coral. The live coral polyps covered the calcareous skeleton of the reef in jellylike masses of emerald green, lime green, and sulphur yellow. Like anemones in miniature, the polyps ranged the entire spectrum of magenta, mauve, and pink.

Down through the clear, distanceless water at reef's edge, the heron could see a large hermit crab. On its tender abdomen it wore the handsome cone of a dark green and pearly-white top-shaped shell. It moved weightlessly over the ripples of sand, temptingly. The shimmer of a wave served to remind the great blue heron that the sea was ever ready to claim him. Waves poured over the reefs on the rising tide, swirled around the slender legs of the wading bird, now and again splashing the fringe of wet plumes that hung from the young heron's spotted breast.

A clap of spray sent the great blue aloft with a leap. He squawked, clutched the air with his powerful wings and wheeled away. His long legs dangled just above the sparkling waves as he slowly flapped off to the rocky point.

Almost all the islanders were now astir. The buses had roared back down into Kingstown. Water had been "headed" up to the houses from the stand-pipe at the bottom of the hill. Likewise on heads the fruits and vegetables for Saturday market in town had come down.

Tourists appeared on the beaches to court precious, even if painful, sunburns. A band of ragged children skipped along, looking for someone to make uncomfortable.

Great blue flew across to the small island just offshore. A small, scaly iguana scuttled off the rocks to the shelter of the bushes. The heron had the beach all to himself. Although the island was the site of a posh resort, what few early rising guests there were seemed to prefer pools created of concrete and painted in shades of Caribbean blue.

Hallelujah! The yard boy dropped a scarlet hibiscus blossom in the plastic basin of sea water and put it on the doorstep so the guests could rinse their sandy feet. Today was going to be a busy beach day. As soon as he finished raking the lawn with his coconut flower-stalk broom, the yard boy planned to join his friends on an Easter outing of their own.

A glossy Antillean grackle swooped in through the open door of one of the cabanas to beg for a crust of toast. Chocolate-brown anoles and smoke-gray geckos ran in and out at will, across the ceilings, across the floors and walls, bringing good luck. A busy little bananaquit slipped in and out through the latticework of another cabana. She was building her purse-shaped nest in the wicker lampshade that hung from the ceiling. A crested hummingbird feeding in the hibiscus hedge glowed green fire, then coal black as it turned this way and that from bloom to bloom.

A slight, energetic man came striding into the yard.

"Hey, Doc!" the yard boy greeted him with a broad smile.

"How ya been, man?" responded Earle Kirby, the island veterinarian. The two men joked and gestured. Then Dr. Kirby headed down to the beach. As his jaunty, shorts-clad figure disappeared beyond a stand of coconut palms, the yard boy grinned and went off whistling to himself.

Doc paused in the palm tree shade to watch a great blue heron fishing on the reef. He marveled when the bird abruptly flickered into motion with a lightning thrust. The bird caught a large fish. With impressive dexterity, it flipped the heavy fish into its beak to swallow head first. The man found himself watching in amazement and laughing out loud as the heron's long slender neck bulged. The heron stalked off on down the reef and the man continued in the opposite direction.

It was a holiday and Doc intended to put in a few hours on his hobby, an extensive collection of pre-Columbian artifacts. He squatted by the bank at the end of the beach to see what the waves had lately uncovered for him: a gracefully flared stone axe blade perhaps, or shards of lovely, rust-red clay pots painted with striking white designs, fragments of footed cassava baking griddles, round sling stones, or bones—anything that might tell him more about the first men in the Caribbean.

As he sat on the beach sifting through the rubble eroded out of the bank, it was easy for Kirby to imagine himself among the Caribs who were there to greet Columbus on the name-day of St. Vincent. Perhaps they launched from this very spot their high-prowed, dug-out canoes and sailed out across treacherous reefs to greet Spanish galleons, the ships that sealed their fate. Or a couple hundred years before that Doc might have feasted on crabs—and passing herons— among the Arawaks. Huge spiny lobsters—clawless, unlike their cold-water cousins—had been easily plucked from the reefs in those days, and sea turtles came often to the lagoon.

The great blue heron, which had been staring into the sea from the reef top, raised its head to study a white plastic bottle floating purposefully in a straight line across the path of the waves. The gliding shape just below the water's surface was a man, the dark tube preceding the bottle his snorkel. The harpoon of his spear gun was tethered to the float. Great blue gave a start and moved to the far end of the reef when the spearfisherman raised his head above the water to take his bearings.

Presently, the diver came ashore with a large, pale fish impaled on his spear. Doc could not resist joining the curious crowd that gathered by the sea wall built in front of one of the resorts. The fish was a puffer. It still had enough life in it to inflate itself into a huge spine-covered globe. The puffer fish made itself larger than the man's head. In the sea, few would-be predators could swallow such a formidable morsel, but its great trick was no defense against this hunter.

The fisherman was not sure whether he would try to eat his catch. Its flesh would be delicious, but its liver and gall bladder toxic. And if he didn't need to eat it, why did he shoot it? Happily no one asked.

No one spoke either about the wall on which they took turns bouncing the gasping fish like a ball. The sand had washed out from beneath and behind the wall. Some time ago a section of the reefs had been blasted out so that bathers need not fear the long-spined, black sea urchins that lived among the coral. Along this "safe" passageway the waves rolled in with nothing to break their force. The pliant sand glowed most attractively under the aquamarine curls of the rollers. But the eroding bank threatened the beachside cabanas, so at low tide men with sledge hammers had pounded up more chunks of the protecting reef, tossed them on the other side of the wall, and cursed the sea.

The commotion was too much for the solitude-loving great blue. He lifted off and circled the cove.

"Pterodactyl," thought Doc as the heron's dark form came banking overhead. The enormous wingspan, reptilian head, sinuous neck, and long legs swept back gave the heron a silhouette that seemed to speak from an ancient unknowable preconsciousness.

Sunlight flashed for an instant on the silvery band on one of the bird's dark legs.

"A banded pterodactyl," Doc chuckled to himself. Someday, he mused, we will know where that heron came from. It will be a good thing when we really know what we're doing with animals, with nature.

There were days when Doc felt like one of the last of the dinosaurs himself. He was keenly aware of the pressures being put on his island by the modern world. The other day he had driven across the island to look at some sick goats, and it had taken hours because crews were repairing the road. As he had sat watching a woman of the highway crew carrying road gravel in a wooden tray balanced on her head he'd thought about where on earth the resources were going to come from for his government to support urgently needed environmental conservation programs.

Great blue headed out across the bay.

"Good luck, my friend," Doc said to himself, and he watched the graceful, powerful poetry of measured wingbeats until the heron was out of sight.

The green turtle made her way accross the reefs.

6
THE CARIBBEAN SEA

EASTER SUNDAY MORNING FOUND the heron heading up the coast leaving behind the coral-rimmed haven of Indian Bay with its golden beaches. Giant rollers twelve feet high at their foamy crests pounded the jet-black volcanic sands of the windward coast. Here and there, like over-turned flowerpots, stood ruins of old sugar mills—towers which once held wind vanes to the never-ending sea breezes. Green valleys, carefully terraced for agriculture, stretched away up into the creases of the mountains. Huge boulders, carved with elegant linear designs long before Columbus came, stared mutely, mysteriously, out over fields of peanuts or arrowroot. Banked fires where charcoal was being made smoldered like tiny volcanoes on the valley walls just below the rim of the forest. Beyond a fringe of silver-foliaged trumpet trees and palms stretched the cloud-bathed forests the St. Vincent parrots called their own.

The Soufrière, St. Vincent's active volcano, sent a column of smoke up from one of the northern peaks. Soon St. Vincent disappeared in the distance behind the great blue heron. The twin cones of the Pitons of St. Lucia, and behind them, the smoking of St. Lucia's Soufrière, rose up in greeting. Making his way up the leeward coast, the heron winged low over the hotel-rimmed bay where Admiral Rodney had once hidden his British fleet by tying palm fronds to the swaying masts. Schooners and banana boats made their way in and out of the busy harbor of Castries. A huge jet swept across the beach and put down at the new airport superimposed on the ruins of old fortifications. The heron did not land.

Fair winds carried the heron past Martinique and Dominica— each island unique as every place on earth is, but each a slight variation on the unifying theme of the whole island chain. Although the heron's journey north would be nothing like the great leap over the Atlantic which had carried him south, the pace of his travels had begun to quicken. West-blowing trades bore him farther and farther to the lee of the island chain, peaks of the drowned Andes of the Caribbean. The sun made colossal sculptures out of insubstantial piles of vapor above the great expanse of the Caribbean Sea.

Late in the day a tiny coral isle appeared, shaped like a footprint, a giant step southwest of Guadeloupe. It was Isla Aves, the coral crown of the Aves Swell, a rise which made its way north four hundred miles across the sea floor from Venezuela. In spite of its position far up in the West Indies, the sandy island was claimed by Venezuela, formerly valued for the wealth of its guano deposits. Unprepossessing as it appeared, it was the last major nesting site in the eastern Caribbean for the green turtle.

The great blue heron fished the windward shallows while handsome black-and-white sooty terns and brown noddy terns wheeled above him in the dusk. The terns shrieked at the tall heron if he walked along their speckled eggs scattered about the merest depressions which satisfied them for nests, so he contented himself with the sand spit at the north end of the island.

Aves was totally devoid of trees. Even those great colonizers of the Caribbean, the coconuts, washed ashore, sprouted, and were washed out to sea again by hurricane seas which regularly swept over the island. The nearest thing to a sheltering shrub or roosting tree was the solitary thirty-foot-tall radar tower on the height of the land. The heron had to make do with that.

Presently the drone of an engine roused great blue. A cargo ship anchored offshore and issued forth a dinghy. Straightaway the men rowed ashore, headed up the beach, and began filling baskets with tern eggs. The fading light seethed with angry terns. Great blue circled up above the pandemonium.

In the lagoon off the opposite shore a female green turtle was making her way across the dark reefs to shore. Laboriously she dragged her huge body up the beach and began to dig the hole in which she would deposit a hundred "Ping-Pong ball" eggs. An exultant shout mingled with the din of the terns as the egg thieves spotted the turtle and rushed to her. She, however, made no sound but a grunting gasp as they flipped her over and struggled to drag her great weight into their dinghy and aboard the waiting vessel.

The shrill crying of the terns continued throughout the windless night. At dawn the breeze freshened; waves lapped farther up the beach. Sooty terns rode the breezes; noddys bowed and wagged their heads up and down at each other. Mother birds searched again and again for missing eggs. The shrieking of an individual would send a whole flock wheeling into the air, sweeping out to sea in a silent circle. Eventually they would settle back, and the business of the colony would go on as before.

The air was already beginning to warm with the new day when great blue resumed his northward journey. Tiny Aves soon vanished behind him. His gray-blue form moved silently, steadily, across mile after mile of dancing, blue Caribbean waters. Cutting diagonally across the upper edge of the Caribbean Sea, the heron left St. Kitts and Nevis, Anguilla and Antigua far to the east. In the crystal-clear waters surrounding the Virgins he came upon a party of scuba divers returning to their anchored schooner. From above they appeared suspended in an invisible medium. Before long the schooner, too, would journey back to the Maine bays for a summer of windjammer cruises.

West along the palm-fringed southern coast of Puerto Rico the heron soared over sunny slopes where the wind sighed in vast seas of sugarcane. A sleek, brown, minklike animal looked up from the iguana it was eating to watch the great bird pass. It was a mongoose: Rikki Tikki Tavi brought from India a century ago to eat the rats that ate the sugarcane. He ate the rats-and then the toads, the snakes and lizards, the birds and their eggs. Mongooses scourged the unique wildlife of the islands. The sugar planters had been dismayed, but there was no way to call their agents back.

Great blue headed on toward the Dominican Republic on the island of Hispaniola. White beaches blinked invitingly at the passing heron. Some of the world's few remaining manatees, homeliest of mermaids, grazed on the beds of turtle grass in the quiet water behind the reefs. Offshore a party of marine archeologists and eager students searched diligently for the coral

94

covered remains of Columbus' flagship. Drum beats rhythmically accompanying toilers in the fields drifted out across the water to great blue. High on the hills, in the shade of mahoganies, men and women picked coffee beans. On the lower slopes they tended tiny garden plots on the lands their forefathers had tilled as slaves.

Departing their winter homes for the season, drawn by some invisible urgency, a large flock of coots followed the heron across the sea. Ahead stretched five hundred miles of brilliant reef-colored Bahama Rise: counting every sand spit with any permanency, each tiny cay and coral islet, some three thousand islands in all—low, flat, and limestone, the fossil bed of an ancient sea.

Mountains of salt, dazzling in the subtropical sun, gleamed alongside the loading docks on Great Inagua. Huge man-made evaporating "pans" glared back at the sun. Where the sea water was channeled into the first of the ponds of ever-increasing salinity, the heron joined a busy company of ducks and cormorants. In the ponds at the other end of the island tall knobby-kneed flamingos paced the shallow waters raking small organisms out of the mud with their upsidedown bills. They fed, loafed on one leg, danced off after one another waving their black-lined wings, squawking loudly. Roseate spoonbills, naked greenish faces peering down their spatulate bills, stirred the mud for small crustaceans and tiny fishes. They marched on past great blue, intently stirring the pot before them. Like the others, they seemed completely indifferent to the presence of the tall blue heron fishing in the deeper channels.

Flocks of ducks passed high overhead; pintails and blue-winged teal were flying north. The young great blue heron took off once more to join them. As he moved along up the islands, he sailed for hours between the blue above and the blue below. He made his way through canyons of clouds with sea-blue floors. Turquoise shallows below him were patterned with pale swashes of sand in graceful free-form geometry.

Calcareous green algae and reefs had done their work forming the sands; the sea had scooped and piled and channeled the sand in a thousand different inventions. Wherever the tides bared the sands in faintest imitation of land, the mangroves had moved in. Their prop roots clutched the sand, stabilized it, enriching it with the wrack of turtle grass, sargasso weed, dead fish and the leaves of the mangrove itself. Spoonbills, ibis, mangrove cuckoos, and whitecrowned pigeons, passing herons, weary tiny migrants—all that rested in the mangrove canopy paid for their perch with their droppings; and the land growing beneath prospered.

Mangroves were not the only land builders. As he flew north, the heron encountered islands whose shapes were different, but the pattern was the same: the looping road planed down the limestone spine of the island, the fringe of elegant homes—or lots scraped out in anticipation—and the keyhole punctuation of slips for the yachts that go with them. Dredge and fill. Wherever man needed a bit more land to fill out his design, he simply scooped it out of the sea.

The young heron flew over the mangroves.

7
THE EVERGLADES

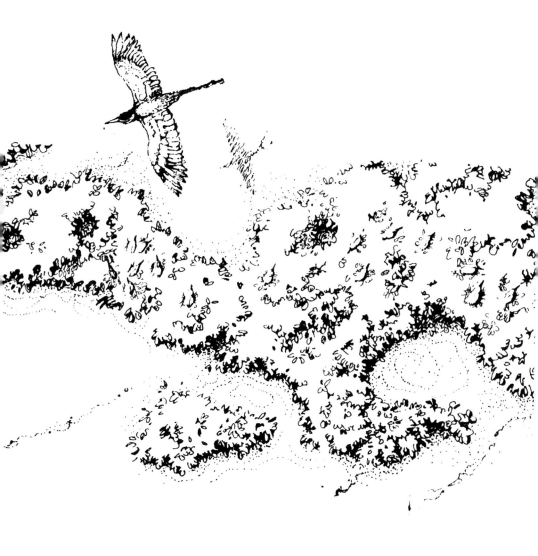

G<small>REAT</small> B<small>LUE</small> W<small>INGED</small> O<small>UT</small> over the deep blue Straits
of Florida where the currents squeezed out between the tip of
Florida and the Bahamas. The dark line of barrier reefs indicated
that the heron was once again approaching land. A white strip of
highway strung green beads of islands together north and south as
far as the eye could see-the Florida keys.

The counterweighted bascule bridge was raised to let a boat
through. The heron's shadow swept over its wake, crossed U.S.
Highway 1 and traveled across the dappled waters of Florida
Bay. No line in the water marked the boundary of the Everglades
National Park, but ahead stretched island after island of pristine
green. For miles the bay was no more than nine feet deep, even at
high tide. A few manatees cruised in the warm shallow waters, a
few crocodiles, and many sharks.

The young heron flapped slowly by the noisy rookery where
young wood storks peered eagerly out through the mangrove
treetops. Roseate spoonbills alighted gingerly on the branches of
their rookery; brown pelicans winged just above the waves bringing
home fish to the young in the mangrove clumps they called their
own. A pair of ospreys had built their shaggy stick nest on a single
ridiculously short young mangrove, but isolation made it safe.

Flocks of dapper, black-and-white skimmers cut lines across the
fishy waters, snapping up fry with the long lower mandibles of their
red scissor bills. Shaggy-plumed reddish egrets dashed crazily here
and there spearing small fish. Great white herons slowly stalked the
shallows, hunting in the manner of great blue himself.

The young heron settled down to feed. Almost at once a school
of silver came flashing by. He struck. The fish was more than he had
bargained for; it wrenched his neck, nearly jerking him off his feet.
Flailing his wings for balance, the heron staggered and splashed.
The flopping of the powerful fish coincided with the heron's violent
head thrusts and the heron was free. Once extricated, he prudently
settled for a smaller fish. A fine mullet slid down his throat. With
the haughty indignation of a dog after a bath, great blue shook the

muddy water from his bedraggled feathers and continued hunting.

Long lines of birds came streaming back to their roosts. The red sun dropped into Florida Bay. Circling above the island-sprinkled bay, great blue beat high into the air. The great dark shape of the heron dropped silently through the warm dusk into the black branches of a quiet clump of mangroves. The rising moon soon bathed the dozing young heron in silver and spread the lapping waters of the bay with its soft sheen. Tired as he was from his long journey, the heron spent a restless night. First there were the clouds of humming mosquitoes. Then a family of raccoons came bustling about beneath his roost, using their clever little hands to pick oysters off the arching roots of the mangroves.

Later in the night the heron saw the coon lead her two roly-poly cubs across the glistening flats to the islet where a colony of white ibis was nesting. He heard the mother coon give an angry hiss, heard her churr at her young ones, and watched them all trot hastily off across the mud. Underneath the ibis lived a rattlesnake that collected the occasional fallen egg or baby bird; its presence discouraged would-be marauders such as the coon family.

Like ghost butterflies several of the restless ibis fluttered their wings in the moonlight. The moon ducked behind some clouds and sleep came at last to the ibis—and a weary young heron.

Stars were winking out; the great sky dome was growing light around its rim as the sun reclaimed the heavens for another day. Car headlights flashed the amber eyes of occasional deer feeding on the grassy roadside swale. Campers, pickup trucks, automobiles— all pulling motorboats on trailers—roared along in the darkness. South they came, down through the vast early morning quiet of the Everglades Park, heading to Flamingo to launch themselves in a day of fishing.

Red lights flashed and blinked in the dawn-dark as one of the vehicles turned into the parking lot at Nine Mile Pond and rolled to a halt at the end of the pavement. A pair of wood storks stalked away down the shore of the glass-calm lake. From the mangroves which formed a cove at the end of the pond came a cacophonous medley of grunts and croaks—the calls of dozens of herons and egrets sitting in the treetops, wading in the shallows.

The car window inched down; a drink can came bouncing, clanging, out upon the pavement. A donut box followed. The phalanx of black vultures parading across the parking lot with outspread wings and measured tread hustled over and settled down to the serious business of bickering over the crumbs.

A camper pulled into the far end of the lot. The couple within admired the way two wood storks exactly bracketed the rising red sun globe. They excitedly identified the knobby, motionless logs floating before them as alligators, and headed their ponderous vehicle on to the next stop of their itinerary.

Flights of ibis crisscrossed the mangroves; mists hung just above the treetops. Shafts of golden light colored noisy herons preening in the branches. A delightful din greeted great blue as he flew down to the lake. He lowered his long legs and settled lightly onto a mangrove beside another great blue. The older bird raised its magnificent set of plumes. The youngster correctly interpreted this as a warning but was unprepared for the ferocity of the thrust which followed. Hastily, he dropped down to the water.

A van pulled into the parking lot. A young woman stepped out and surveyed the lake shores with her binoculars. She stood a long time watching the oriental loveliness of the tall white egret fishing alone on the opposite shore with only the "S" curve of its own reflection for company. Trim gray slacks and the embroidered patch on her shirt sleeve identified the girl as Park Service personnel. Her name was Elaine. On the seat of the van was her hat which looked like Smokey the Bear's. She would be wearing it later in the day when the sun grew fierce.

Elaine frowned when she saw the trash on the pavement. As she picked up the plastic rings of a six-pack carrier she thought of the heron she had found dead on the shore-strangled in the twists of plastic rings wrapped around its slender throat. She pictured the men in powerboats who tried to run down water birds for sport. Such people were the only part of her job she didn't like.

From the back of the van Elaine pulled a long-handled wand. She paused a moment smiling at an anhinga which had caught a bass and brought it to the shelter of the sedges near shore to swallow. The anhinga knew it was being closely watched. Vultures and a heron were waiting for it to drop its tasty catch. With aid of neither hands nor feet, the bird had to maneuver delicately with its bill to turn the fish head first down its gullet without dropping it for an instant. An alligator came cruising over as if to offer aid.

The girl eyed the gator as attentively as did the anhinga. An older ranger had told her the only alligators he feared were the "tame" ones—the ones which had lost their fear of man. The man's knowledge she did not doubt—he had spent all his young years in the swamps as a poacher.

With a quick flick of the wand Elaine grabbed the floating can that was her quarry. An alligator that swallowed a can—and they not infrequently did—was doomed to a horrible, painful death.

A car pulled up alongside Elaine as she returned the wand to the van and was anxiously scanning the sky for signs of rain. It was the end of the dry season; the glades were parched; wildlife concentrated at the few remaining water holes such as this one. The acrid smell of smoke which had crept up was from a controlled burn she knew, but it was a touchy time for the Park Service. Some people liked to set fires of their own.

The family that had emerged from the automobile interested Elaine. She loved to play detective with the tourists. To set a good example she leaned into her van and got her Smokey hat.

It was the large, clear plastic parabolic reflector and microphone that the man carried which interested her. He was wearing headphones and recording sounds with what looked like state-of-the-art equipment. What a glorious honking medley he was getting as herons called in treetops, whirled overhead, and squabbled in the shallows!

The children listened intently as Elaine explained why fire is necessary to maintain the plant associations characteristic of the Everglades. They told her about the cattle egrets they had seen on the way down: The birds were patrolling the edges of the fire, snapping up insects fleeing the flames.

They talked about the recorder, about film, and about cameras. Elaine's face glowed as she told them of the photos she had taken in her time off: of courting little blue herons, the one nibbling the other's shoulder feathers, and a great blue with a four-foot-long corn snake in his mouth. Her prize was her picture of a pair of great egrets with their bills clamped together in a "kiss" that was really a clinch as the female coped with the male's aggressive response. And the large flock of snowy egrets parading and fanning their lacy plumes! Oh, she loved the Everglades.

One of the boys pointed excitedly to the great blue heron flying over their heads. They could clearly see a band shining on its leg. A banded bird…that meant someone had once held the heron. And one day the numbers on the bird's leg might be read again.

Elaine drove off, singing to herself. Sometimes she wondered what animals had ever done to deserve people, but then came moments such as this when she felt brimming with the joy of human existence, ecstatic in the sensory richness of participation, delighted with the privilege of being a part of it all.

Miles of Everglades shimmered in the heat. Below him the young great blue heron heading north had seen the blue-and-green mosaic of mangrove islands in Florida Bay give way to a labyrinth in which the green came to predominate over the blue.

Finally the water had been replaced entirely by a vast expanse of gold. The tree-clad, tear-shaped islands were moored in a sea of saw grass. *Pa-Hay-Okee* the Indians called it—the River of Grass. More than a hundred miles to the north the waters of Lake Okeechobee began their journey to the sea across the great, flat, tilted sheet of limestone that is south Florida. In the rainy season, waters had flowed through the saw grass less than a foot deep. The current of this fifty-mile-wide river would scarcely be apparent to man, but a heron feather would float, ever so slowly, south.

Cracked baked mud—parched pale gray—was all the heron found now. He saw the furrowed tracks that marked where alligators had dragged themselves along in search of precious water. On the highway, several turkey vultures were picking over the remains of a hapless diamondback rattlesnake which would go searching no more. Its once-handsome pattern stretched part way across both lanes of the roadway.

To escape from the blinding noonday sun the great blue dropped down into one of the islands of trees—a hardwood hammock. Perched in a fragrant pond-apple tree growing in a solution hole in the limestone near the center of the hammock, the heron gradually became aware of the creatures in the shady dark of this other world. Bright green anoles scampered up the gnarled limbs of the live oak tree which dominated the hammock. Air plants bristled like giant shaving brushes along its limbs; curled up knots of resurrection fern huddled on the tree waiting for the spring rains; tiny yellow orchids cascaded from the hoary branches where golden orb spiders hung their magnificent webs.

In the wisps of Spanish moss—another of the pineapple's air plant kin—a parula warbler was feeding. One of the birds that watched great blue last summer from the lichen-draped spruces of the Maine islands? Other northerners were sharing the hammock: a ruby-throated hummingbird, several phoebes, and a Baltimore oriole on its way home from Central America. The live oak itself was at the southern edge of its range, surrounded by tropical species that had reached the northern edge of theirs: wild coffee, a small mahogany, and the pillarlike royal palm that towered over all.

When diagonal shafts of sunlight illuminated the dark zebra butterflies fluttering on silent wings through the shadowy spaces, the young heron left his cool napping place. As great blue beat up above the tree island he saw thunderheads piling up on the horizon, empty clouds that would bring no relief to the thirsty land. His strong wings carried him along a ridge crowned with Caribbean pines. Heat waves radiated up around the fans of saw palmettos creamy with froths of blossoms. A resinous fragrance of pines baked by the sun wafted up to the passing bird.

In the saw grass distance bright banner leaves indicated the presence of a water hole. Poachers called the plant alligator flag. Where it grew there was deep water; where there was deep water, an alligator had thrashed out a pool and piled up a huge nest for her leathery eggs. The heat of the rotting vegetation joined with the potent sun to hatch tiny, wriggling, squeaking, yellow-striped baby alligators.

The heron alighted amid the flag and white arrowhead blossoms on the edge of the pool. Out in the deeper water floated yellow spatterdock, delicate water lilies, and even a tangle of insect-trapping bladderwort. The sky-blue heron fishing among the dark blue spikes of pickerel weed felt at home although this pool had been scoured out by gators rather than the glaciers of the north. Like an arrow on a drawn bowstring, the head of the heron poised just above the water.

Fishing was excellent. The pool teemed with mosquito fish. Around the sterns of the saw grass and other emergent vegetation was a sleevelike coating of yellowish algae. So rich with microscopic animals and larvae of insects and other creatures are these mats — perhaps a hundred kinds of creatures—that scientists lumped them all together calling the whole association periphyton, or "plant wrapper." Upon the periphyton grazed the small fish which in turn fed the larger fish, on up to the long, needle-nosed gar fish. The gars dined on young alligators if they could, and in turn had to avoid being consumed themselves by the larger gators.

The large pancake form of a soft-shelled turtle carne gliding by. Now and then it poked the flexible tip of its snout above the water like a snorkel. Glossy, blue purple gallinules walked about the lily pads. Another great blue heron stepped out of the tall vegetation to fish at the edge of the open water. A cottonmouth moccasin went swimming across the water's surface and a short-eared little marsh rabbit paddled swiftly off through the watery grasses.

On glowing white wings a great egret swooped over the pond, skillfully plucked a fish from the water, and settled gracefully atop a willow to have dinner.

An airplane dropped from the sky and buzzed low over the water startling the fishing herons. The egret gave a loud squawk and winged off in the opposite direction. Two alligators which had been sunning nose to nose on a log slid off into the water. Huge, immobile reptiles all across the pond turned their inscrutable

The heron found the fishing excellent.

gaze upon the intruder. The gators could see the men as the plane banked above them, the time warp awry, mechanical marvel clattering over creatures of the warm, wet Mesozoic. And the men saw the alligators. Every one.

Out on the highway the Park Service van pulled off to the side of the road. Elaine leaned out and peered hard in the direction of the plane. Poachers? Uneasiness gripped her; her veins ran hot. She sped up the highway, jerked the van abruptly hard right, and bumped along a dusty track that led off into the glades from the highway.

As if taking advantage of the distraction, one of the great blues that had been fishing the open waters marched over to a jumble of floating vegetation and grabbed up a tiny squeaking baby gator. A sound like a Mack truck shifting down roared across the water hole. Perhaps in answer to the challenge of the plane that was disappearing in the distance, a bull alligator began to bellow. From another cove came an answering roar.

Alligators in the Everglades.

Great blue could see the gator raise its head above the water weeds. From its inflated throat pouch the noise poured forth. Water dripped off the gator's horny brow and the long yellow teeth of its monster grin. Every fiber of the bird's being resonated with the deep sound.

From her sheltered vantage point Elaine could pick out a third alligator answering from its corner. A huge gator, perhaps the first one, pushed across the water and sank in a swirl beneath the vegetation. Another gator pushed off and similarly disappeared. The two erupted with a violence that threw weeds, water, and baby alligators into the air. Their writhing bodies and powerful tails sent spray after spray arcing above the dark water.

As abruptly as it began, the interaction ceased. The two sank once more and oozed off in different directions. Had the young heron recognized Elaine as the girl he had watched this morning

at Nine Mile Pond? She thought she had recognized him—a young bird, and she was fairly certain she had glimpsed the flash of a band as the long leg disappeared in another step. She had meant to keep her eyes on him but she wasn't sure just which bird it was when she turned back from watching the big gators. There he was now, perhaps. Just grabbed one of the tiny baby gators.

Smash! The heavy jaws of an enraged mother gator crushed down upon the heron. As Elaine watched, horrified, the alligator's powerful jaws ripped apart the big bird. In seconds it was just blue feathers and bleeding flesh destined to disappear down the leathery maw, heron of the skies no more.

The elemental show as over. The quiet of the Everglades seemed to ring in Elaine's ears. She stood a moment. Then she turned and walked slowly back the little path through the saw grass.

At the gator hole a young snapping turtle was finishing the bits of flesh on the heron leg it found among the water lilies as the sun went down. A curved gray feather floating lightly on the water cast a delicate shadow on the sun-gilded surface. It rocked gently in the ripples as a swimming otter raised its sleek head briefly to look around. Another of south Florida's spectacular sunsets lit up the western horizon. Long needles of slash pines etched black lines across the gold. The floating feather moored fast against a blade of saw grass and darkness fell.

Flocks of ducks sped by in the night: lesser scaups and ring-necks headed for Hudson Bay, the potholes of Saskatchewan; shovelers, pintails, blue-winged teal—all headed north.

When morning came they were all gone. The skies belonged to the wood storks and egrets. The great blue herons that nested at the northern edge of the park headed off to the sloughs and canals to fish for their young. Red-shouldered hawks blinked in the lazy morning sun, surveying the glades from the tops of bald cypress trees just leafing out in feathery green.

Whereas hardwood hammocks and pines grew wherever the

limestone gained an altitude of two or three feet—pines where fires pruned away the hardwoods, hammocks where flames were held at bay—the saw grass sea was punctuated by yet another tree formation. Cypress heads, or domes, claimed the moist depressions of the bedrock.

The waters flowing across the vast limestone pan were rich in dissolved calcium salts. The algae of the periphyton in the river of grass precipitated the calcium, died, and became marl. This limey ooze which covered great blue's feet to such a great depth when he had fished in Florida Bay formed a meager skin over the bedrock of the glades. But it was enough to support higher plant life.

When these plants died and decayed, enough acids were produced to etch hollows in rock: sink holes in the hammocks, saucers in the saw grass. And the bald cypress came in, creating their own special world. Prickly pineapplelike bromeliads and delicate orchids sprouted from their slender trunks. Long veils of Spanish moss hung from the cypress branches and swayed gently in the wind. Huge and handsome ferns perched around the knobby knees that the cypresses sent up from their roots.

The great blue heron fishing quietly in the cypress-bordered canal that paralleled the Tamiami Trail at the north edge of the park was up to his knees in the key element in the fate of the Everglades, of the adjoining region known as Big Cypress, of all south Florida: water.

The road bed itself was borrowed from the ditch that became the canal. The Tampa-Miami highway not only opened up the west to loggers and land exploiters, it interrupted the flow of the grassy waters from Lake Okeechobee to the Everglades. Centuries of saw grass turned to peat had formed rich muckland just waiting to be drained and turned into fields of celery and beans. Lake Okeechobee didn't always stay where it belonged in a hurricane, so levees and dams had been built to protect the farms which the engineers had created.

An armadillo scuttled across the highway and disappeared in the grass. A spotted sandpiper teetering on the canal bank fluttered away as an elderly black couple set up their chairs, took out long bamboo poles, and settled down to fish. The noisy yellow school bus rumbling down the highway crossed the sluice gate and squeaked to a halt at a small plank bridge across the canal. Two small, dark-eyed children tumbled out. A slender teenager stepped down. The young Seminole stopped on the little bridge for a moment and looked at the pall of smoke across the western sky. He watched as the heron before him eased forward a single step. The Indian kicked at a fossil clam shell in the white path and ambled off through an avenue of palmettos to his home—the same kind of thatched-roofed, open-sided chikee that his forebears had learned to make when they fled to these swamps from their native Georgia more than two centuries ago.

Without a ripple, time seemed to flow past the heron poised immobile.

Canada geese grazed the frozen marsh.

8
THE ATLANTIC FLYWAY

NORTH, NORTH WITH EVER increasing urgency flew the young great blue. The southern coast fading behind him was geologically mature, its coastal plain sloping gradually to the sea. As it is everywhere around the world, the meeting of land and sea was a dynamic one: rolling cylinders of waves pushed up ridges of sand before them, beach grasses quickly laced dunes together, and barrier islands formed as the grasses held the land together long enough for beach heather and dusty miller to get a foothold and be followed by shrubby bays and hollies, and finally, wind-pruned oaks or pines.

But the sea never missed a chance to take back its gift. The beaches were ranked with jetties where man tried to argue with sea—usually, ultimately, in vain. Time and again the sea moved the beaches, breached the dunes, cut new channels, rearranged the real estate.

The quiet lagoons of the great network of estuaries that formed behind the barrier beaches were laced with twists and tangles of silvery water courses. This was the path the great blue herons followed. Countless flocks of water birds traveled the narrow trail on the edge of the vast continent: the great Atlantic Flyway.

Live oaks hung with Spanish moss; beaches offering up pearl-lined pen shells , lavender-blue Portuguese man-of-war jellyfish floats drying in the sun, blown west over the "cold wall" of water that lies between land and the warm Gulf Stream: That was Georgia and South Carolina. And birds flew overhead, both night and day.

Moon shells and surf clams, wrecked ships' timbers and treacherous fogs off Cape Hatteras—graveyard of the Atlantic-where the cold currents meet the Gulf Stream, that was North Carolina; and the drowned rivers where ocean invited itself into Chesapeake Bay: Virginia, Maryland and Delaware.

On pressed great blue. Over huge areas the sea, like a sheet of vinyl, was stained and fingerprinted with the spills of a careless painter. Dark sludge underlay the water for miles. Pools in the tidelands glowed vivid green, wild purple, lurid rust. However, not all the colors were poison. Yellow and brown blotches on the sea sometimes showed where a plankton bloom was underway. The dense, cold waters which sank in the winter had begun their spring upwelling, carrying precious nutrients up to the surface where the microscopic plants of the ocean could flourish on them. The sun smiled longer each day on the phytoplankton. The tiny animals of the zooplankton likewise responded with a population boom. Spring had come to the sea.

In the streams of the salt marshes, snowy egrets stirred the waters with their bright yellow feet and clapped their bills on the larval eels that swam by. The eels of the Atlantic had all been born in the Sargasso Sea. Their eggs floated in the depths beneath the seaweeds, hatched into elvers that looked like tiny leaves of glass, and spent the first half year of their lives riding up the coast cradled in the warm flow of the Gulf Stream. In a dramatic change that baffled men for years the young eels, tiny dark rods, headed up the streams that fed the sea to spend their adult lives in fresh water. Great blue paused to refuel himself on the swarming elvers or adult eels whenever he could, even though eating a three-foot-long adult eel meant a battle. A long eel thrashing about his neck left the heron mud-stained and dripping, but full—after some ten minutes or more of swallowing.

The closer great blue came to his birthplace and home for a scant half of the year, the greater distances he traveled. Maine herons leap-frogged over populations of birds of their own kind already well established in their nesting. Indeed the aggressiveness of these birds was no invitation to linger. Faster, faster. On to the north.

Only a cold front blasting down from the north could stop the migrating waves of birds, forcing them to put down wherever they were. At such times the destinies of enormous numbers of birds hung in the balance. Traveling all together gave many species the advantages of increased protection from predators, and perhaps the benefit of pooling their navigational capabilities, but it also meant that cruel, freakish weather conditions could wipe out a very high percentage of the population.

113

The young great blue had safely traversed one of the densest concentrations of mankind on the face of the earth, stretching from Washington to Boston. Scarcely had he left the great sandy hook of Cape Cod behind him than April sent one last winter storm to make fools of men and birds alike.

The heron sought shelter in the lee of some beach plums behind the dunes that gave Plum Island its name. A howling northeaster sent huge rollers crashing down upon the beach, sand stinging through air, waves scudding across the protected waters of the salt marsh that stretched between the island and the shore.

Great rafts of scaup ducks bobbed unconcernedly in the lagoons. Some had preceded the young heron from the ponds they had fished together in the Everglades; others had wintered here. All would be headed back to the Arctic as soon as the storm subsided. Hundreds of black ducks had settled on the clam flats, heads turned into the wind. Ducks seemed to be everywhere. Even in the stormy ocean flocks of golden eyes and long-tailed ducks rode the cold and angry gray Atlantic.

Gnarled branches groaned protestingly in the wind. Beach grasses traced wild circles in the sand around them. A great egret flapping in to shelter disappeared like a wraith, its pale plumage enveloped in a whirl of white. The yearling heron felt his first touch of snow. Wind ruffled the long feathers on the young heron's back, fingers of cold prying into his being. Great blue turned to face the blast.

By noon of the next day the storm had abated; the sun shone wanly overhead. Canada geese grazed the frozen marsh; the tall, dark heads of the birds standing sentinel appeared above the swaying grasses. Far from shore the great blue saw flocks of canvasbacks. Their long bills gracefully echoed the elegant curves of their slender heads. Their backs flashed neatly white; the heads of the males glowed burgundy.

Blue-billed scaup floating closer to shore echoed a modified version of the full-dress formality of the canvasbacks. But it was little goldeneyes that stole the show. The dapper little drakes bobbed and bowed; they stood lip on the water with beating wings sending showers of icy spray flying. They rocked back, tilted their heads back till their bills pointed straight to the heavens, and opened their mouths in a gulping motion to send forth their squeaky call of love.

Blow away, you snows. Spring has come!

Great blue hurried on his way.

The heron winged gracefully over the dark spruces.

9
MAINE

HERONS, HERONS, HERONS; EVERY day more birds appeared in the spruces on the tiny island in the Maine bay. Fitting into the social order of the colony, visiting familiar haunts, establishing his fishing grounds, the young great blue heron just completing his first round trip found it an exciting time.

On land, honeybees buzzed in the pussy willows. Song sparrows sent their exuberant melodies trilling over muddy streams of melt water that coursed through the fields on their way to the sea.

A young mother followed her two daughters who were skipping in the spring sunshine down the path to the cove. As she took off her mittens to untie the rope that held the skiff at the wharf, she caught sight of a tall blue heron silently surveying them from the far shore.

Her little girls clambered into the skiff, their cheeks glowing almost as brightly as their orange life jackets, and they rowed out to their motorboat. On its bow proudly bobbed the wooden marker painted with the colors of her own lobster-pot buoys. The young woman had lived all her life on the hill above this cove. She loved the outdoors. Her husband was a fisherman. Why should she not also make time in her life to be out on the bay she loved so well, she had asked. And so he had given her some traps of her own.

As their little boat headed out to the mouth of the cove, she pointed out the great blue heron to her daughters.

"I'm so glad to see him back," she said as she snugged the rubber apron around her coat and struggled with the wet rope that brought the first lobster trap to the surface. They hauled the trap onto the bow deck. Like treasure hunters the girls picked brittle starfish, a sea cucumber, a lobster, and two crabs from the slatted interior.

The heron lifted off and winged gracefully over the dark spruces.

"Look, he has a band on his leg. He's one of ours!" the older girl announced triumphantly. Their friends, the boys whose father studied the birds, had showed them bands, told them heron stories, and had even taken them for a picnic on the smelly island at the end of last summer.

"I expect it is," the woman answered, readying fresh bait. "But you'd have to catch it and read its number to be sure," she laughed.

Then she stopped, rested her hands on the dripping trap, and watched the great bird flap across to the other side of the cove. What a lot of the world that bird has seen, she mused. Her husband always fitted his boat out to go shrimping or scalloping in the winter, but this year she had been able to persuade him to take a week off to drive to Florida and back. Her own little girls, they had been as far south as Massachusetts.

"Mumma, where has the heron been?" the littlest girl asked.

The woman watched the disappearing bird in thoughtful silence. She dropped the lobster trap back into the water with a splash and shook her head.

"He went south for the winter, dear," the woman said softly.

Acknowledgments

THE AUTHOR FOLLOWED THE flight paths of the great blue herons in a variety of aircraft, ranging from a sardine spotter in Maine and twin engine Islander in the West Indies, to 747's across the oceans. Warmest thanks for advice, cooperation, and inspiration go to the following, with their affiliations identified as they were at the time of my writing: to Dr. Kenneth L. Crowell, ecologist at St. Lawrence University; David B. Wingate, Chief Conservation Officer, Bermuda; Dr. I. A. Earle Kirby, Veterinary Officer, St. Vincent; Dr. Edward L. Towle, president, Island Resources Foundation, St. Thomas, U.S. Virgin Islands; Richard ffrench, author of the Guide to the Birds of Trinidad and Tobago; Dr. Thomas E. Lovejoy, World Wildlife Fund; Alexander Sprunt IV, National Audubon Society; the Bird Banding Laboratory of the U.S. Fish and Wildlife Service; Dr. Douglas Mock, University of Oklahoma specialist in heron biology; and Dr. Timothy Williams and his wife Janet, Swarthmore College biologists whose radar network of island weather stations and ships at sea documented the Bermuda Flyway.

Nature Notes

READERS WHO HAVE TRAVELED this far with the great blue heron probably are interested in all the regions from Maine to the Caribbean. Very likely those of us who love herons have personal heron observations to share. At the time of the first publication of *Great Blue*, birders were invited to contribute data to the Colonial Bird Register, a joint project of the Laboratory of Ornithology at Cornell and the National Audubon Society Research Department, in cooperation with the U.S. Fish and Wildlife Service. The computerized data system for collection and dissemination of information concerning colonial water birds recognized the need for serious amateurs to help in collecting data for expanding our knowledge of colonial species. Over half the cooperators were amateurs. Citizen scientists can provide invaluable environmental data for identifying areas of concern and generating environmental impact statements. The North American Nest Record Card Program, also part of the Cornell Data Records Program, found that 85 percent of its contributors were amateurs. NestWatch is the current nest-monitoring project developed by the Cornell Lab of Ornithology in collaboration with the Smithsonian Migratory Bird Center. Since the demise of the Colonial Bird Register at Cornell University, no national colonial waterbird population database currently exists, but planning is underway to develop such a resource.

The Cornell Laboratory of Ornithology offers a wealth of information for the beginning birder as well as for the advanced aficionado. It would not be overstating to declare that the Laboratory of Ornithology and its web site demonstrate superbly the great potential benefits of the digital age and the Internet era.

Laboratory of Ornithology
www.birds.cornell.edu

Cornell University
159 Sapsucker Woods Road
Ithaca, NY 14853
Telephone: (866) 989-2473, toll-free

Great blue herons range over nearly all of North America, nesting from Alaska to the Yucatan. They use all the major flyways—the Pacific, Central, Mississippi, and the Atlantic Coastal Flyway. Some herons may winter only slightly south of their summer range while others go all the way to South America. The Nature Conservancy has acquired for protection a number of heron rookeries and feeding areas throughout the United States. This private organization acquires land to be preserved for its natural, aesthetic, and scientific values, often in cooperation with a local educational institution, conservation group, or a local, state, or federal government agency. Volunteers may be active in local projects or state chapters. The mission of The Nature Conservancy is to preserve the plants, animals and natural communities that represent the diversity of life on Earth by protecting the lands and waters they need to survive. In the years following the original release of this book, TNC has increasingly focused its work on large bioregional projects, and the rising land trust movement has taken over acting on the local scale.

The Nature Conservancy
www.nature.org

4245 North Fairfax Drive
Suite 100
Arlington, VA 22203
Telephone: (800) 628-6860

The island in Penobscot Bay where this story begins and ends has now received the protection of a conservation easement held by Island Heritage Trust. As civilization encroaches on available habitat, herons rely more and more on protected lands. Great blue herons are colonial nesting birds and it is imperative that they continue to find safe havens for their rookeries. Land trusts are admirably filling that role in Penobscot Bay as well as elsewhere. They deserve your support.

Island Heritage Trust
www.islandheritagetrust.org

PO Box 42
Deer Isle, ME 04627

Office: Heritage House
420 Sunset Road
Sunset, Maine
Telephone: (207) 348-2455

Maine Coast Heritage Trust
www.mcht.org

Main Office: 1 Bowdoin Mill Island
Suite 201
Topsham, ME 04086
Telephone: (207) 729-7366

Did you know that we in the Penobscot Bay region are also blessed with an outstanding local chapter of the Audubon Society? Your membership check (individual $35) not only helps promote environmental education and advocacy, but you simultaneously become a member of National Audubon Society and Maine Audubon as well as the Downeast chapter. You will receive Maine Audubon's *Habitat:The Journal of Maine Audubon*, and the wonderful *Downeast Audubon Newsletter* that tells you about local field trips, tours, children's programs and discounts at nature stores and sanctuaries nationwide. Every May the Downeast chapter cosponsors a special weekend of events to celebrate the return of the spring migrants, a wonderful way to meet the birds and the people who love them.

Annual Wings, Waves & Woods Weekend
www.deerislemaine.com
and
www.islandheritagetrust.org

Maine Audubon Society
Downeast Chapter
PO Box 1212
Ellsworth, ME 04605

Maine Audubon Society
www.maineaudubon.org
Headquarters/State Office
20 Gilsland Farm Road
Falmouth, ME 04105
Telephone: (207) 781-2330

SPECIES LIST

1. MAINE

great blue heron	*Ardea herodias*
common raven	*Corvus corax*
American robin	*Turdus migratorius*
red-winged blackbird	*Agelaius phoeniceus*
Canada goose	*Branta canadensis*
black-throated green warbler	*Dendroica virens*
yellow-rumped (myrtle) warbler	*Dendroica coronata*
northern parula (warbler)	*Parula americana*
common eider	*Somateria mollissima*
great black-backed gull	*Larus marinus*
osprey	*Pandion haliaetus*
cormmon tern	*Sterna hirundo*
double-crested cormorant	*Phalacrocorax auritus*
green sea urchin	*Strongylocentrotus droebachiensis*
moon jelly	*Aurelia aurita*
green crab	*Carcinides maenas*
common periwinkle	*Littorina littorea*
dog whelk	*Thais lapillus*
barnacle	*Balanus balanoides*
blue mussel	*Mytilus edulis*
brittle star	*Ophiopholis aculeata*
northern starfish	*Asterias vulgaris*
herring gull	*Larus argentatus*
monarch butterfly	*Danaus plexippus*

meadow vole (mouse)	*Microtus pennsylvanicus*
mink	*Mustela vison*
green frog	*Rana clamitans*
whirligig beetle	*Gyrinus spp.*
barn swallow	*Hirundo rustica*
white-throated sparrow	*Zonotrichia albicollis*
snapping turtle	*Chelydra serpentina*
sand dollar	*Mellita testudinata*
common razor clam	*Ensis directus*
littleneck clam	*Mya arenaria*
clam worm	*Nereis virens*
common northern moon snail	*Polinices heros*
herring	*Clupea harengus*
mackerel	*Scomber scombrus*
ruddy turnstone	*Arenaria interpres*
black-bellied plover	*Pluvialis squatarola*
sandpiper	*Calidris spp.*
harbor seal	*Phoca vitulina*
Atlantic harbor porpoise	*Phocoena phocoena*
Wilson's storm petrel	*Oceanites oceanicus*
common puffin	*Fratercula arctica*
finback whale	*Balaenoptera physalus*
rorqual (sei whale)	*Balaenoptera borealis*
humpback whale	*Megaptera novaeangliae*
common blackfish (pilot whale)	*Globicephala melaena*
great egret (common, American)	*Casmerodius albus*

2. BERMUDA

sergeant major fish	*Abubdefduf saxatilis*
Bermuda skink	*Eumeces longirostris*
cahow	*Pterodroma cahow*
white-tailed tropicbird	*Phaethon lepturus*
European goldfinch	*Carduelis carduelis*

132

land crab	*Gecarcinus laterallus*
Gulf fritillary butterfly	*Agraulis vanillae*
green sea turtle	*Chelonia mydas*
mallard	*Anas platyrhynchos*
blue-winged teal	*Anas discors*
mosquito minnow	*Gambusia affinus*
kiskadee	*Pitangus sulphuratus*
house sparrow	*Passer domesticus*
yeIIow-rumped warbler	*Dendroica coronata*
black-throated green warbler	*Dendroica virens*
northern parula	*Parula americana*
starling	*Sturnus vulgaris*
bluebird	*Sialia sialis*
Jamaica anole	*Anolis grahami*
giant toad	*Bufo marinus*
zebra periwinkle	*Littorina ziczac*
baby tooth snail	*Nerita* spp.
common West Indian chiton	*Chiton tuberculatus*

3. THE SARGASSO SEA

whimbrel	*Numenius phaeopus*
flamingo	*Phoenicopterus ruber*
Atlantic bottle-nosed dolphin	*Tursiops truncatus*
humpback whale	*Megaptera novaeangliae*
green sea turtle	*Chelonia mydas*
Atlantic hawksbill turtle	*Eretmochelys imbricata*
Sargassum fish	*Histrio histrio*
Sargassum crab	*Planes minutus*
Sargassum barnacle	*Lepas spp.*
Sargassum shrimp	*Latreutes fucorum*
white-tailed tropicbird	*Phaethon lepturus*

4. TRINIDAD

mangrove crab	*Aratus pisonii*

133

termite	*Nasutitermes spp.*
fiddler (gundy) crab	*Uca major*
mangrove oyster	*Ostrea frons*
scarlet ibis	*Eudocimus ruber*
blue-winged teal	*Anas discors*
little blue heron	*Egretta caerulea*
snowy egret	*Egretta thula*
Louisiana heron	*Egretta tricolor*
great egret	*Casmerodius albus*
magnificent frigatebird	*Fregata magnificens*
cattle egret	*Bubulcus ibis*
black-crowned night heron	*Nycticorax nycticorax*
brown pelican	*Pelicanus occidentalis*
common tern	*Sterna hirundo*
anhinga	*Anhinga anhinga*
tilapia	*Tilapia mossambica*
pigmy kingfisher	*Chloroceryle aenae*
yellow-throated spinetail	
(rooti)	*Certhiaxis cinnamomea*
dickcissel	*Spiza americana*
common potoo	*Nyctibius griseus*
great kiskadee	*Pitangus sulphuratus*
ruby-topaz hummingbird	*Chrysolampis mosquitus*
common emerald (copper-rumped)	
hummingbird	*Amazilia tobaci*
feruginous pygmy owl	*Glaucidium brasilianum*
channel-billed toucan	*Ramphastos vitellinus*
crested oropendola	*Psarocolius decumanus*
bushmaster (mapepire)	*Lachesis muta*
rufous-tailed jacamar	*Galbula ruficauda*
blue-crowned mot mot	*Momotus momota*
cocoa thrush	*Turdus fumigatus*
collared trogon	*Trogon collaris*
red-legged honey creeper	*Cyanerpes cyaneus*
black-faced antthrush	*Formicarius analis*
bearded bellbird	*Procnias averano*

mountain (manicou) crab	*Kingsleya* spp.
rainbow tree boa	*Epicrates cenchris*
common black (crab) hawk	*Buteogallus anthracinus*
tree frog	*Phrynohyas zonata*
blue-gray tanager	*Thraupis episcopus*
silver-beaked tanager	*Ramphocelus carbo*
violaceous euphonia (semp)	*Euphonia violacea*
jaçana	*Jacana jacana*
common gallinule	*Gallinula chloropus*
barn swallow	*Hirundo rustica*
blue-and-white swallow	*Notiichelidon cyanoleuca*
rufous-breasted hermit hummingbird	*Glaucis hirsuta*

5. ST. VINCENT

flying fish	*Dactylopterus volitans*
magnificent frigatebird	*Fregata magnificens*
elkhorn coral	*Acropora palmata*
fire coral	*Millepora complanata*
staghorn coral	*Acropora cervicornis*
long-spined sea urchin	*Diadema antillarum*
rock-boring sea urchin	*Echinometra lucunter*
marbled chiton	*Chiton marmoratus*
West Indian brittlestar	*Ophiocoma echinata*
baby tooth snail	*Nerita* spp.
chain moray eel	*Echidna catenata*
speckled crab	*Grapsus grapsus*
sergeant major fish	*Abudefduf saxatilis*
four-eyed butterfly fish	*Chaetodon capistratus*
sea anemone	*Condylactis gigantea*
barnacle	*Chthamalus tisus*
magpie shell	*Cittarium pica*
iguana	*Iguana iguana*
carib grackle (Lesser Antillean)	*Quiscalus lugubris*

bananaquit	*Coereba flaveola*
Antillean crested hummingbird	*Orthorhyncus cristatus*
anole	*Anolis trinitatis vincentii*
gecko	*Hemidactylus turcicus*
West Indian spiny lobster	*Panulirus argus*
checkered puffer fish	*Sphaeroides nephelus*
St. Vincent parrot	*Amazona guildingii*

6. THE CARIBBEAN SEA

great egret	*Casmerodius albus*
brown noddy (tern)	*Anous stolidus*
sooty tern	*Sterna fuscata*
green sea turtle	*Chelonia mydas*
small Indian mongoose	*Herpestes auropunctatus*
manatee	*Trichechus manatus*
American coot	*Fulica americana*
roseate spoonbill	*Ajaia ajaja*
wood stork	*Mycteria americana*
flamingo	*Phoenicopterus ruber*
snow goose	*Chen caerulescens*
pintail goose	*Anas acuta*
blue-winged teal	*Anas discors*
mangrove cuckoo	*Coccyzus minor*
white-crowned pigeon	*Columba leucocephala*

7. THE EVERGLADES

manatee	*Trichechus manatus*
American crocodile	*Crocodylus acutus*
wood stork	*Mycteria americana*
roseate spoonbill	*Ajaia ajaja*
brown pelican	*Pelicanus occidentalis*
osprey	*Pandion haliatus*
black skimmer	*Rynchops niger*

reddish egret	*Egretta rufescens*
great white heron	*Ardea herodias occidentalis*
striped mullet	*Mugil cephalus*
white ibis	*Eudocimus albus*
glossy ibis	*Plegadis falcinellus*
raccoon	*Procyon lotor*
coon oyster	*Ostrea frons*
black vulture	*Coragyps atratus*
American alligator	*Alligator mississipiensis*
anhinga	*Anhinga anhinga*
corn snake	*Elaphe guttata*
great egret	*Casmerodius albus*
snowy egret	*Egretta thula*
turkey vulture	*Cathartes aura*
eastern diamondback rattlesnake	*Crotalus adamanteus*
green anole	*Anolis carolinensis*
golden orb weaver	*Nephila clavipes*
northern parula	*Parula americana*
ruby-throated hummingbird	*Archilochus colubris*
eastern phoebe	*Sayornis phoebe*
northern (Baltimore) oriole	*Icterus galbula*
zebra butterfly	*Heliconius charitonius*
mosquito fish	*Gambusia affinus*
short-nosed garfish	*Lepisosteus platyrhincus*
southern soft-shelled turtle	*Trionyx ferox*
purple gallinule	*Porphyrula martinica*
eastern cottonmouth	*Agkistrodon piscivorus*
marsh rabbit	*Sylvilagus palustris*
Florida snapping turtle	*Chelydra osceola*
lesser scaup	*Aythya affinis*
ring-necked duck	*Aythya collaris*
northern shoveler	*Anas clypeata*
pintail duck	*Anas acuta*
nine-banded armadillo	*Dasypus novemcinctus*
spotted sandpiper	*Actitis macularia*

137

red-shouldered hawk	*Buteo lineatus*

8. THE ATLANTIC FLYWAY

stiff sea pen	*Atrina rigida*
Portuguese man-of-war	*Physalia pelagica*
common northern moon shell	*Polinices heros*
surf clam	*Spisula solidissima*
snowy egret	*Egretta thula*
eel	*Anguilla rostrata*
Barrow's goldeneye	*Bucephala islandica*
long-tailed duck (oldsquaw)	*Clangula hyemalis*
great egret	*Casmerodius albus*
Canada goose	*Branta canadensis*
canvasback	*Aythya valisineria*
greater scaup	*Aythya marila*

9. MAINE

northern sea cucumber	*Cucumaria frondosa*
lobster	*Homarus americanus*

138

COLOR PHOTOGRAPHS

ABOUT THIS BOOK

IN 1979 A U.S. SUPREME COURT decision upheld an IRS ruling that warehouse stock could not be depreciated for tax purposes unless the stock were also reduced in price or destroyed. The IRS subsequently clarified its policy to apply to publishing companies. So Great Blue essentially had its wings clipped before it had a chance to fledge: the Times Books stock and the plates were destroyed and the rights were transferred back to the author. In ensuing years, publishing has evolved significantly, with e-books and high quality, short run digital printing enabling authors to use technology to distribute their work in quite new ways.

ABOUT THE AUTHOR

NATURAL HISTORY WRITER Marnie Reed Crowell majored in biology at Randolph-Macon Woman's College and received the M.S. in Biology from the University of Pennsylvania.

Her first book, Greener Pastures (Funk & Wagnalls 1973), was excerpted in Readers' Digest, widely quoted, anthologized, and used in rural studies courses at St. Lawrence University. Marnie has written many articles appearing in magazines such as Redbook, Natural History, Down East, and Readers Digest. She hosted and produced the award-winning North Country Storytelling Festival series for National Public Radio at WSLU-FM. Her book North to the St Lawrence, used in 7th grade social studies classes in New York, was subject of a three part television series for public television.

When her ecologist husband Ken retired from teaching at St Lawrence University, they moved to Maine, the site of his 40 years of summer research on the islands of Penobscot Bay. Quick Key to Birds was produced to aid re-starting Audubon Christmas counts on Deer Isle. Like the Quick Key to Moths and Butterflies, it benefits the local conservation commission.

Artist who practices meditating, Hospice volunteer and active conservationist, Marnie was called upon to practice what she preached after a moonlit ice skating accident in 1999 left her with a Traumatic Brain Injury. Marnie described the process of healing in her novel,

The Coast of May (Threehalf Press 2010). She turned to the power of nature, meditation, and art as sources of courage and healing. When her recovery was well under way she wrote many poems that she wanted to publish with photographs of the area's wild places. At about the same time, photographer and clinical psychologist Dr. Ann Flewelling contacted Marnie about the meditation classes Marnie was offering on behalf of the Island Medical Center. The two subsequently formed Threehalf Press, dedicated to using new media to produce art that speaks for the environment.

Commissioned to write a poem for the opening of the Penobscot Narrows Bridge, Marnie also pairs her poems with essays and Flewelling photographs in Beads and String, a Maine Island Pilgrimage (Threehalf Press 2008), produced for the benefit of Island Heritage Trust. Shared Light, Images of Penobscot Bay and Shore Lines are also Threehalf Press collaborations. Island Meditation (Threehalf Press 2011), originally crafted for the local medical center, pairs Marnie's lessons on meditation practices with Flewelling's photographs.

Marnie Reed Crowell's poems accompany Audubon prints in the Maier Museum of Art at Randolph College. A Sky of Birds, Downeast images (Threehalf Press 2011), with bird photographs by chapter members accompanying her poems, benefits the Downeast Chapter of Audubon.

Handsome illustrations from the original version of Great Blue are by Mary Champenois, an artist whose long and illustrious career specialized in wildlife and birds of prey. Mrs. Champenois, now retired, studied and banded raptors in Pennsylvania, and she lives in New Jersey.

To see more of Marnie Reed Crowell's work, visit:
www.threehalfpress.net.

ILLUSTRATION CREDITS

Line drawings:
Mary Champenois

Photographs:
Front cover | Marnie Reed Crowell
Back cover | Kenneth L. Crowell

NORTH top left and right | Ann Flewelling
NORTH bottom left | Leslie Clapp

SOUTH top | Charles Zelnick
SOUTH bottom left | Marnie Reed Crowell
SOUTH bottom right | William McHenry

Cover design:
David Allen